THE TAO

(((O F)))

SURVIVAL

JAMES MORGAN AYRES has served with the 82nd Airborne Division and the 7th Special Forces Group, worked as a consultant for U.S. government agencies and private corporations, founded four companies, and lived and worked all over the world. He's written seven books, taught seminars on the Tao of survival and related subjects, and has been a student and teacher of Asian thought, martial arts, healing, and meditation for more than forty years. He currently lives in Southern California. Visit his Web site at www.jamesmorganayres.com.

THE TAO
(((OF)))
SURVIVAL

SKILLS TO KEEP YOU ALIVE

GIBBS SMITH
TO ENRICH AND INSPIRE HUMANKIND

JAMES
MORGAN
AYRES

First Edition
17 16 15 14 13   5 4 3 2 1

Published by
Gibbs Smith
P.O. Box 667
Layton, Utah 84041
1.800.835.4993 orders
www.gibbs-smith.com

Designed by Andrew J. Brozyna
Printed and bound in Canada

Gibbs Smith books are printed on either recycled, 100% post-consumer waste, FSC-certified papers or on paper produced from sustainable PEFC-certified forest/controlled wood source. Learn more at www.pefc.org.

Library of Congress Cataloging-in-Publication Data

Ayres, James Morgan.
  The Tao of survival : skills to keep you alive / James Morgan Ayres. —
1st ed.
    p. cm.
  ISBN 978-1-4236-3231-3
1. Survival. 2. Disasters—Psychological aspects. 3. Emergency management—Psychological aspects. 4. Taoism. I. Title.
  GF86.A97 2013
  613.6'9—dc23
                        2012038524

For ML, better angel of my heart.

CONTENTS

ACKNOWLEDGMENTS

We all stand on the shoulders of those who have gone before us and those who have supported us. I owe debts to many and offer my thanks to all of these people for helping to make this book possible: Katie, for the gift of life; Marylou Ayres, for patience and dedication, for traveling the long road with me, for love and a life worth living; Ashley Ayres, for pointing the way back to the path for a traveler lost in the deep forest; my family, for their support and for making it all worthwhile; Cheryl Carter-Runnels, for being the first to believe and for years of work and faith; Joseph Shields, for professional advice and direction, for constancy and loyalty, for friendship and faith beyond the call, for showing by example the meaning of the word "brother"; Beth Esculano Yüken, for sunshine and sanctuary, for open-hearted friendship and a wonderful place to work; J, for dedicated reading of a first draft and perceptive and incisive comments; Ayse Dağıstanlı, who by gentle persistence persuaded me to teach yet another class, and by doing so reminded me what students need most; Robin Munson, for continuing inspiration, great personal insights and encouragement; Art Munson, for professional support, friendship and for being there at a critical moment; Tom Negrino, for his continuing advice and for setting an example of grace under pressure; and Chris Wilton and Karen Fox, for creating a lovely refuge and inviting us to share it, for friendship, incisive comments, good conversation and wine.

I have studied and trained with too many teachers to list them all. Noteworthy for their pivotal teaching are: Kenny Wong, whose intervention in a street fight set me on a path that took me to a back room in a Chinese restaurant, to kwoons, temples, monasteries, rooftop and back-alley training centers, to Hong Kong, Taiwan and meetings with extraordinary men; Uncle Wong, who first showed me the true power of the Tao and Kung Fu, and that there were things under the sun I had never dreamed of; Lao Chung Li, who taught me the core of the Tao and was a good friend in a hard place; Guro Dan Inasanto, who accepted me into his private training, and taught me a unique perspective on martial arts and skills that has served me well; Guro Emilano Vasquez, who stood with me back to back; and Sifu Andre Salvage, for his teaching in San Soo.

Special thanks for healing and helping to put my body back together to Sifu and Doctor Kam Yuen; and for healing and meditations to Sifu Carl Totten.

This is a better book due to the work of the people at Gibbs Smith: Bob Cooper, an editor whose perception, engagement and professionalism are all that any writer could hope for; Andrew Broyzna, for insightful and creative design work; Suzanne Taylor, whose creative decisions were critical to making this the book it is; and Mr. Gibbs Smith, an old-school gentleman, all too rare in today's world, whose vision and wisdom I admire.

Last, but never least, to Paul Levine, for counsel and patience with an impatient writer.

FOREWORD

It is not every day that one comes across a gem. And that is exactly what this book is. For anyone who is into survival—that is, into life and living—then this book is truly a precious commodity to be read by everyone.

I am a longtime practitioner of survival, not only as an instructor, but as a way of life. So when I read this I was well pleased to see so much of what I have learned from years of training and come to believe from hard-gained experience all brought together so well and so concisely as Morgan has done here.

It is as if this book can save you twenty years of dirt time, to learn the greater lessons of survival—one's self. It is not the physicality of rubbing sticks in one's environment that matters most, but rather the mental ability to use one's wits and will to master their situation that often decides the day, and that's what this book does for the reader. It gives you the foundation and the structure upon which all can be built.

Morgan also has studied many Asian arts, which have a way of focusing on transcending the seemingly most immediate to seeing past them, and as a result, finding a better solution to the immediate. I too have found these lessons on the path of learning and studying many martial arts, primarily Aikido, and found they perfectly align with the needs of every survivor.

In addition, Morgan is a Special Forces brother from a generation before me. The wars and names are different, the lessons are not. One must face themselves, their fears and their real threats in order to overcome them. No amount of wishing them away will save the day.

His book is fused with practical tips that are useful, and suggestions that can benefit everyone. *The Tao of Survival* is also very practical in that there are many TTPs (tactics, techniques and procedures) in the form of simple exercises anyone can execute and would serve all of us to implement. Even the most seasoned among us would do well to read and review these wonderful concepts.

In this way and in his book, Morgan has blended all the tried-and-true lessons of combat, studies of the arts and teachings of primitive skills to make one of the most important books on the subject of survival—that book full of the common sense that we often find so uncommon in life.

It is therefore with the highest regard and recommendation that I support James Morgan Ayres's book, *The Tao of Survival.*

—Mykel Hawke
author of *Hawke's Green Beret Survival Manual* and Special Forces combat commander (www.mykelhawke.com, www.specops.com)

INTRODUCTION

The scent of free-floating fear permeates the zeitgeist like last week's grease in a fast-food joint. We live with economic catastrophe, tsunamis, tornados, earthquakes, floods, nuclear plant meltdowns, terrorist attacks, never-ending wars and violent criminals. We know the media seeks out disaster, thereby ratcheting up anxiety and making everyday life feel as dangerous as a tour of Afghanistan. But the media doesn't create the events—they simply report them.

We live in a mobile, fast-moving world, a world where most people travel for business and pleasure and can find themselves in an "Oh my God" situation far from home; a globalized world where we're all connected and anyone from anyplace can show up on your doorstep; a world where almost anything can happen—and often does.

The police bust a sex slave house in a nice suburb—yours—and the bad guys make a run for it—through your living room. You're driving to work, stop at an intersection and find yourself in the middle of a gangbanger shoot-out. A big rig flips on the freeway and you're roused from your commuter coma by ten tons of fast-moving machinery coming at your windshield. You're hot, bored and annoyed, standing in line for a ritual groping before boarding your flight, when you hear loud noises and you're thinking, "Could those be gunshots?" and uniformed people with submachine guns run past you yelling, "Down, down, down!" You take that adventure trip, rafting down a river in Costa Rica, and your raft capsizes; your guide hits his head on a rock and now you're on the riverbank with an unconscious guide, most of your gear swept away and no idea what to do next. You're in a taxi coming from the airport in Bangkok, jet-lagged from your twelve-hour flight, and you wonder, "Why is my driver turning down this alley, and who are these guys with the machetes?"

All of these things are part of everyday life—for someone. Disaster is common. Disaster is normal. Everyday life presents survival situations as real as a heart attack in the shower. Life is, and always has been, dangerous and ultimately fatal. No one gets out of here alive. We'd all like to delay our exit as long as possible, but living in a bunker, or in abject fear and constant anxiety, isn't much of a life. The Tao—the way—is to enjoy and live life to the fullest while being aware of and prepared to deal with its exigencies.

"Survivor" television shows proliferate. We know they're mostly entertainment, but we watch closely for wilderness survival tips. Various survival manuals sell well, as do novels featuring survival themes, and for good reason—we live in tumultuous times. We all know it and many of us are trying to get a handle on how to better take care of ourselves in an all-too-likely emergency.

The primary focus of *The Tao of Survival* is real-world, core survival skills that can save your life in an emergency situation—anytime, anyplace. These skills benefit both men and women and have nothing to do with the stereotyped image of the survivor as a muscled, cigar-chomping, camo-wearing hero with a big knife and machine gun. Can you keep your head when all others have lost theirs and are running, screaming and trampling each other to get to the exit? Would you like to possess the calm of a Special Forces soldier in a firefight, the focused attention of a fighter pilot coming in for a nighttime landing on an aircraft carrier, the threat-evaluation skills of a covert operator in a high-threat zone? Do you know what to do if your hotel is on fire and you're on the twentieth floor and your spouse has been overcome by smoke? Do you know how to spot a potential terrorist or violent criminal?

Many today are concerned about the collapse of the worldwide economic system, the possibility of societal breakdown, or how to take care of their families and cope with natural disasters—floods, earthquakes, hurricanes and tornados. The fundamental Tao skills in this book will help you in planning, and enable you to make the right decisions and deal with these extreme events, all of which were common occurrences in ancient China when this body of knowledge was developed.

The skills that you can learn from *The Tao of Survival* not only improve your chances of survival, they also empower you in practical ways and can enhance your enjoyment of daily life. Become more tuned in to your environment and you'll not only pick up on threats before they go critical, you'll see clouds with the eyes of a child again, smell flowers you hadn't noticed before, and hear birds in the park a block away. These skills can also enable you to become more sensitive to your body and head off illness before it gains a foothold, find your ideal body weight and be comfortable with whatever level of physical activity you choose to stay fit.

The Tao of Survival is unlike any other book on survival. Research, real-world experience and statistics clearly show that in a life-threatening emergency nine out of ten people—both men and women, including many who have had standard survival training—are unable to act effectively to save their lives or the lives of their loved ones. Read this book, practice the exercises, acquire the skills and become part of the 10 percent. Then pass on these skills and work towards turning that 10 percent into 100 percent.

AN APPROACH TO SURVIVAL

There are other books, some of them good books (I list a few in the "Suggested Reading" section in the back of this book), that go deep into wilderness survival, primitive skills, disaster preparedness and other situation-specific preparedness. This is all useful knowledge, but these skills are not foundational to staying alive in a crisis.

Knowing how to rub sticks together to make fire won't help you when a building is collapsing around you. Having two weeks supply of food and water at home won't do you any good on a hijacked plane. Your end-of-the-world Hummer loaded with supplies might help—the guys who have stolen it from your parking lot, that is. This is not a book about "survivalism," guns, Rambo knives, stockpiling military rations or wearing camouflage. Nor is it about fearmongering or buying into the Terrorist Derangement Syndrome now afflicting the United States.

This is a book about personal empowerment and the ability to survive and flow with life's vicissitudes. As flight attendants tell us, when the oxygen masks come down put on yours first before trying to help another. If you are not able to help yourself, you cannot help others. If we first begin with ourselves, we can then help our loved ones to survive. Then we can reach out and help those in our immediate community and even others in distant lands—a subject I address in the Afterword.

Virtually every survival book starts by counseling its readers not to panic, to focus on evaluating and solving the immediate problem, to be adaptable, to press on when losing heart. None of them tell you how to acquire the states of mind and emotional controls that are necessary to accomplish these things. The acquisition and development of these mental and emotional skills, and other powerful mind/body skills, are the primary focus of *The Tao of Survival*.

The conceptual base for certain of these skills originated with Taoist philosophy, science, meditation, mind/body skills and martial arts. These concepts and skills have now been translated into practices compatible with the Western temperament and have been taught to elite military personnel, covert operators and others who work in high-threat zones, and to many ordinary people who wish to improve the quality of their lives and their odds of survival.

A SHORT OVERVIEW OF TAOISM AND ITS PRACTICES THAT RELATE TO SURVIVAL

Tao is pronounced *Dao*. Tao translates as: the way, the path, the underlying principle and natural flow of the universe.

As China is the mother culture of Asia, Taoism is the fountainhead of Asian philosophy and science. Early Taoism was devoted to determining the foundational principles of our universe by observation, analysis and reflection. From this study, over centuries flowed meditation methods, Traditional Chinese Medicine, health practices such as Chi Gung, many martial arts, Feng Shui, and practical skills useful in everyday life and in extreme survival conditions. Taoists approach life and all of its pleasures and problems by being in harmony with the way, the natural flow of the universe, the Tao.

Taoism has its roots in prehistoric shamanism. As Chinese culture developed, the concepts of Tao also developed. When Buddhism arrived from India, certain elements of it were combined with Taoism and transformed into Chan Buddhism, a spare and stripped-down version centered around Taoist concepts and skills. Chan was exported to Japan, and translated became *Zen*. Zen is better known in the West due to many Japanese teachers coming to the West after World War II with the specific purpose of teaching Zen to westerners. D. T. Suzuki, perhaps the best-known Zen teacher in the West, said, "To understand Zen you must understand the Tao." Due to the inward-turned nature of Chinese society in the West, Chan and Taoism remained a practice confined for the most part to the Chinese community.

In the early decades of the People's Republic of China, Taoism was suppressed. During the Cultural Revolution, people who practiced any form of Taoism, including martial arts, were actively persecuted. Taoism, and its principles, martial arts, and medicine, continued to flourish in the rich environments of Taiwan, Hong Kong and Chinese communities in the West and throughout the world. But until recently Taoism was little known outside the Chinese community. The Chinese are not by nature proselytizers.

Over centuries, branches of Taoism took on certain external artifacts and aspects of religion: priests, rituals, formal worship at temples and so on. But in its purest essence Taoism is highly individualistic, not institutionalized or ritualized and not a religion of any kind. In this book I do not address any aspects of any of the religious branches of Taoism.

From its inception, Taoism was primarily a philosophy and early form of science, with the goal of understanding and describing the nature of all things in the universe, the universe itself, man's relation to the universe and how man could best interact with the world around him. At its core, Taoism emphasizes living in harmony with the basic principles of the universe. Certain Taoist fundamental principles have become well known in the West; for example, yin and yang—the concept that for every thing there is an equal and opposite thing: light and dark; hard and soft; heat and cold; joy and sorrow. The seminal work of Taoism is the *Tao Te Ching,* attributed to Lao Tze.

The Warring States Period in China, from the fifth century BC to the second century BC, was a time of almost constant warfare and disruption. During this period Sun Tzu wrote the classic *The Art of War,* which is firmly grounded in Taoist principles, strategy and tactics. Kingdoms fell and people were forced to flee their cities and homes with little more than they could carry. They learned to be ready at all times to "leave through the eastern gate." "Leaving through the eastern gate" has become known as a philosophical and spiritual concept, but like much in Taoist thought has a practical application. During these centuries of war, unrest and societal chaos, Taoists developed an extensive body of work focused on the practical aspects of individual and group survival in tumultuous times. It is this aspect of Taoism on which *The Tao of Survival* is focused.

BEING AWARE, READY AND ABLE

In action, be aware of the time and the season.
—Tao Te Ching

Survivors all have certain things in common—they're aware of their surroundings, informed about conditions in their environment, ready to react as the situation requires, able to determine the right action and capable of acting effectively. Some reactions require a split-second response, others careful analysis. Both depend on the quality of information received, the inner decision-making process and the ability to react. This book begins with lessons devoted to developing awareness, sensory input, decision-making processes, fundamental mind/body survival skills and developing the ability to react effectively to a given situation, and continues with practical applications and other survival skills.

Many people in today's society go about their daily affairs without even being awake, let alone aware or ready. Go to any public place and watch people. You'll see the unaware—eyes glazed, flip-flops flapping, shuffling along, slack bodied and sucking on Slurpees. What if there's a minor earthquake, just enough of a tremor to break the plate glass windows into shards and send them flying across the mall. Do those folks look like survivors to you? Think they'll duck and cover in time to avoid being shredded by razor-sharp glass?

How often do you see people crossing intersections, totally unaware of traffic, bopping along plugged in to their iPods? Would they notice a truck bearing down on them with failed brakes and horn blowing? In effect those people are Audio Zombies and unaware of their surroundings. Are they survivors?

You're walking down the sidewalk. Ahead of you is a young family—Mom, Dad and a toddler, a cute little girl. The toddler runs ahead and then quickly darts off the sidewalk and into the path of an oncoming car. Dad springs from a walk to a sprint in a split second. But his slick, leather-soled shoe slips and he falls to the pavement. He was aware, but not ready. Can he recover in time to save his daughter?

What if your child was walking a few feet ahead of you on a perfectly safe sidewalk, happy and absorbed in eating an ice-cream cone. You hear screeching tires, turn to look and see a car heading for the sidewalk, right at your child. You run ahead, grab your child, spin and jump out of the path of the car. Could you have done that if you were wearing flip-flops? What if you were wearing earphones and listening to music? Would you have heard the car coming?

A friend, a Special Forces soldier who was usually aware, ready and well able to take care of himself, was once hit from behind by a drunk with a pool cue. He was knocked unconscious and beaten severely. When I visited him in the hospital where he was being treated for his injuries, he said, "I never saw it coming." He had had a couple of drinks and was talking to a woman he had just met, and had developed tunnel vision and an acute case of target fixation.

A few years ago there was an earthquake in Japan, and as a result a tsunami fifty feet high was predicted to hit Santa Monica, California. If it hit, this tsunami would wipe out everything for a half mile inland—the pier, malls, apartments, homes. All would be destroyed by this cataclysmic wave. Twenty minutes before the tsunami was predicted to hit, a television reporter at the pier interviewed some of the people in the crowd that had formed. The reporter asked people why they were there, risking their lives. Many said they wanted to "see the big wave." One young woman told the reporter that she had come "to see the big salami." Avoiding this life-threatening situation didn't require a split-second decision or lightning reflexes, simply the ability to process information, be aware of a danger and act prudently. As it turned out, the tsunami lost its power in mid-ocean and caused no damage. What if it had hit with the force predicted? Would the people at the pier have survived?

Our first goal is to insure you will be aware and ready at critical moments and have the information and ability to react to save your life and the lives of your loved ones. With practice, the mind/body skills you learn will become habits and operate below the level of conscious thought.

Here are some examples of states of mind that can get you killed, and that show the primacy of mental states to survival.

FIGHT, FLIGHT, FREEZE OR FLAP

Everyone has heard of the fight-or-flight reaction, the response that is coded into our species DNA and enables us to survive immediate threats. We perceive a threat and our bodies shift into fight-or-flight mode, and we do one or the other, whichever is situation appropriate. However, there are two other responses that are far more common among nonsurvivors: freezing and flapping.

Freezing is a primary response to an unfamiliar situation, also known as the "deer in the headlights" effect. An example of it can be seen in an amateur video of the Olympic Games in Atlanta in 1996. A bomb exploded and everyone in the crowd froze, then milled around doing nothing useful while drifting towards the loud noise. Fortunately there was not a terrorist with a command-detonated bomb waiting for the crowd to coalesce. Staying frozen can get you killed. People will remain frozen when they don't have a clue how to deal with a situation, often until it's too late. Like the deer in the headlights, you're toast if you don't have a situation-appropriate response.

People also flap. This is a term I first heard from a British SAS soldier discussing a firefight. To *flap* means to move fast and frantically doing irrelevant things but nothing that will help the situation, kind of like a hog on ice—lots of squealing, legs and hooves every which way but no forward motion. Indecision can be just as deadly as not having a clue.

LEARNED HELPLESSNESS

Many people died during the tragedy of 9/11 because they obeyed the public-address system in their offices, which told them to stay at their desks. Believing that "everything was under control," they waited until it was too late to get out and died. One security officer, a veteran Special Forces soldier, told his people to ignore the public address system, believe the evidence of their own eyes and ears, and get out of the building. Those people survived.

Our society promotes the notion of "letting the responsible authorities take care of it." Doing so can get you killed. The passengers who attacked and overwhelmed the would-be "underwear bomber" saved themselves and everyone else on the plane. What would have happened if they had waited for the Air Marshal to solve the problem—the one not on board? You are the authority when it comes to your own survival.

BUILDING BLOCKS

Teachers open the door. You enter by yourself.
—Ancient Taoist proverb

We begin with foundational survivor's skills: *centering*—coordinating mind and body; *directed attention*—focusing and concentrating on an object, task or the mind/body; *visualization*—seeing things in your mind's eye; and how to enter *Tao space,* also known as Zen space or the Zone. This is a state of mind/body connectedness where you have superior coordination and perceptive abilities. These terms will be explained in more detail before we begin the lessons.

In the primary lessons, as you learn to center, to direct your attention, to develop visualization abilities and to enter Tao space, you will develop and sharpen all of your senses—the five we are all familiar with: sight, sound, scent, taste and touch; and the sixth, which most of us use whether we're aware of it or not: perception. Have you ever felt someone staring at you from behind or from a distance, before you saw them with your vision? How did you do that? What was it you felt, "eye rays"? Most of us also feel, to a certain extent, "vibes" from people and places. What are those vibes?

Current research, including evidence from neuroimaging studies, shows that each of us (and all living things) generates an electromagnetic field, and that concentrated directed attention generates different brain-wave patterns that can affect this energy. Taoist adepts have for centuries identified this energy as *chi.* Much of classic Taoist practice is devoted to developing, maintaining and directing chi, which is regarded as our life force. Although we will touch on directing chi for health in the section on self-healing, fuller exploration is a subject for a future book on which I'm now working: *The Tao of Heath, Diet and Well-Being.*

I think of chi and vibes simply as energy. In these exercises you will learn to develop your perception and awareness of energy, and to develop your powers of observation, concentration and visualization. Doing so improves the quality of your sensory input, and therefore improves the quality of your intuition and decision-making ability, which in survival situations is critical. We will develop application skills as we build these foundational exercises. These exercises build on basic survival skills you have developed from the time you were an infant, skills that are inherent in all of us but have for most become blunted by the nature of our daily lives.

Some situations require a split-second reaction. In a survivor, sensory input, intuitive evaluation and action will blend seamlessly in a split second. Other situations require a considered, carefully thought-out response. The same process of sensory input will feed both intuition and analysis. In either instance your odds will improve with the quality of your input. Once learned, the skills operate more or less automatically, although you might need a refresher if you allow your skills to get rusty.

Once developed, you will be able to use these abilities not only in an emergency but in everyday life: to see a person's face and be able to read it deeply and understand the person behind the face and their intentions; to feel and evaluate the vibe of an unfamiliar and potentially threatening situation; to scan a crowd and spot a troublemaker (if there's one present) before they act; to perceive a sunset in a way that moves you deeply; to feel joy in everyday life and wonder at the world we live in.

We begin by developing each sense separately. By working on each sense individually we can better develop them and be able to use them to their fullest. Later lessons focus on bringing all senses together and using them in concert to provide full and accurate information about anything, anyone or any situation on which you focus. By doing so, you provide your instincts, intuition and analytical mind the information required to enable you to reach a split-second decision or develop a detailed course of action. We will also build on those skills to coordinate input and judgment with action, and to develop mental and physical skills to work in close harmony so they become mind/body skills. Although this might sound like a lengthy process, and the individual steps must be learned one at a time, once acquired this process can, and often does, take place in a microsecond.

Many of the skills taught in this book have by tradition been closely held and taught only to initiates and only face-to-face. Even then the instructions were opaque and required the student to puzzle out meaning and methods. Only when the student made significant progress did the teacher offer detailed guidance. That is how I learned.

When I began this training many years ago, the Taoist adept whom I learned from required me to center and hold center and to direct my attention to one thing for extended periods, usually hours. His instructions were oblique, requiring me to figure out the meaning and details of his teaching, which he would confirm when I got them right. Most of my other instructors taught in the same way. This was, and is, a method passed down over centuries, one that has been proven effective—at least for highly motivated and dedicated students who are also able to devote themselves to virtually full-time study. However, this approach is not workable for most people.

The Tao of Survival is a break with that tradition in that it openly and clearly explains processes and provides details on how to learn certain skills and how to apply them in the world outside the training hall. It is also a break with traditional teaching in that the methods taught do not require years to master. My motivation for breaking with tradition comes from standing at the grave sites of many loved ones who might have lived longer if they had even a minimal mastery of these skills, and to bring potentially lifesaving skills to those who cannot afford the time to learn them in the traditional way.

Contemporary research has shown that disciplined directed attention for shorter periods can produce results similar to extended concentration. The lessons in this book are clearly explained, and the exercise format has been developed for people in our modern world who have many demands on their time.

At first glance, ancient wisdom and practices might seem irrelevant to survival in the modern world. Practice the exercises and you will soon see they are as useful and important today as they were two thousand years ago. On the surface many of the lessons seem quite simple, and tedious. You might think it would be boring to stare at a flower. But it is not—if your mind is fully engaged. Further, the lessons lead to subtle and powerful abilities.

The lessons can be demanding, but they reward directed attention and perseverance. The committed student will discover a wealth of new experience and develop critical skills, possibly lifesaving skills. Basic competency in these skills, as they are taught in this book, is no more difficult to achieve than learning to drive a car well enough to pass a driver's test, and can be acquired with minimal work. High-level expertise will require more practice. Anyone can drive, but not everyone can compete in Formula One.

Note that these skills, like many others, are best learned by "no action," a Taoist concept that means no stress or striving. Approach and do these lessons in a relaxed manner. Let them come naturally. If you do not find immediate success, don't try harder. Simply do them again in an easy, relaxed way and let the skills develop naturally.

LESSON FORMAT

Each skill development lesson follows a similar format. However, some are timed and some are not. Although it's best to do an entire lesson in one session, it is not necessary to do so to gain the benefits.

The beginning lessons that are timed each require a little more than thirty minutes, and consist of an initial seven-minute exercise to be repeated three times; a three-minute exercise to be repeated three times; a one-minute exercise to be repeated three times; a ten-second exercise to be repeated three times; and finally a one-second exercise to be repeated three times. Certain later exercises, after you have acquired the basics, will be of shorter duration—much shorter. Others will be longer.

If you have difficulty finding a free thirty- to forty-minute block of time in your day, you could, for example, do the initial seven-minute exercise before breakfast, the second seven-minute exercise after lunch, the third seven-minute exercise before dinner, and the three-minute exercises, one-minute exercises, ten-second and one-second exercises before retiring for the night.

One of my students with a very high-pressure life (the CEO of an international corporation, and the father of three children) pressed a flower from his garden in his notebook to use as his object of attention (more on objects of attention below) and did the exercises during spare moments in his busy day.

Try to do one lesson a day, if possible a new lesson every day—if you've mastered the previous day's lesson. If not, review the previous day's lesson before going on. It's important that each lesson is mastered first in order to build on it. Continue to do one lesson each day until you've done all the lessons in this book. Approach these lessons in this way and the skills you've learned will transform into base-level abilities that you can perform automatically. You'll be able to keep these abilities honed by daily use. If, for whatever reason, you allow these abilities to become rusty from lack of use, go back to the basics and you'll find the skills will return quickly.

Read through the instructions carefully, make sure you understand them, then put aside this book and do the practice. Do the lessons in the order they are presented. Do not skip ahead. Each lesson builds on the ones that preceded it. Only by doing the practice will you acquire the skills. Reading about them isn't enough.

You might find some of the exercises to be boring. You might enjoy them. Many, if not most, turn these exercises into enjoyable games and invite friends and family to play the games with them. Whatever you may feel about the lessons—do them. They are necessary to the survivor.

DEFINITIONS

CENTERING

Centering, in terms of the Tao, and for our purposes, means to bring together mind and body. If you follow the instructions on breathing and directing your attention and intention, centering, for the purposes of these lessons, takes place naturally. Being centered is a prerequisite to all lessons and is key to survival. There are many classes on meditation that teach centering in a quiet, calm environment, but few ever take their lessons to the real world. This will not do for the survivor. To avoid the states of mind that lead to panic and ineffective action, you must learn to be centered in a survival situation. As you progress and practice, you will learn to center and remain centered, not only while sitting calmly at home or in a meditation hall, but during crises and high-stress activity. The person who remains calm while others panic is centered. Centering is the opposite of being scattered. Be centered and you will not freeze or flap.

TAN TIEN

Don't panic. You don't have to learn Chinese. **Tan tien** is one of the few Chinese terms I'll use, and I use it only because there is no equivalent word in English. Your tan tien is a spot just below and behind your navel—a notional spot, not a physical organ. Visualize your tan tien as a balloon the size of a grapefruit that inflates and deflates as you inhale and exhale. This spot, this visualized balloon, is your center of balance, of energy, of your physical and energetic body. It is as important as any physical organ.

CHI

Chi is the energy, or life force, present in all things and flowing freely throughout the universe.

TAO SPACE

Following the lessons in this book will enable you to get into **Tao space.** There are levels in Tao space, some leading to deep and focused meditations and insights, levels where an hour can pass like a minute. For our purposes we will focus on the active level, a place where time seems to slow down; where you can "take your time in a hurry"; where you see, hear and perceive everything with clarity; a place where your mind and body are fully coordinated and you know the right action. This is a state of mind familiar to fighter pilots, combat soldiers, top athletes and shooters, advanced martial artists and Taoist adepts. Some naturals find their way into this space as they grow and develop. The rest of us can learn how to get there. Tao space is a mind/body state you want to cultivate. Tao space is survivor's space.

BREATHING

In many of the exercises in this book you will need to use specialized **breathing** designed to aid in focusing, directing your attention, centering and developing energy. Breathing might seem like a simple thing, too simple to bother with. After all, you've been breathing all your life without thinking about it. But breathing correctly is at the center of this training and a foundational survival skill. Pay attention to doing this kind of breathing in your basic exercises, and as you progress it will become automatic.

ENERGY DEVELOPMENT AND ATTRACTION

Generated by the earth, the sun, the entire universe, and present in air, water and earth, **energy** surrounds us at all times. By using the methods in this book you can learn to attract energy from these sources, develop it within and use it to help others and yourself. Of course you also get energy from food, a different kind of energy.

DIRECTED ATTENTION

Directed attention is a state of mind/body, and a process by which you focus and concentrate your mind, and in some instances your senses, on one object, purpose or situation. Once learned, you can direct your attention to *see* deeply into a person and determine their intentions, to sense cues that signal danger, to pick out and hear a hummingbird's wings in the shrubbery next to a busy street with traffic noise all around. When focused inwards, directed attention can mitigate pain, heal or help to heal illness and injury, modify your biochemistry and enhance physical conditioning.

INTENTION

Intention is the purpose that drives your attention and the energy behind it. When you look at a flower are you admiring its beauty or considering whether you can eat it? Intention is also related to will and purpose. A clear purpose and intention will help you learn the lessons in this book. Powerful intention will enable you to push through what you think are your body's limitations and help you to survive when the body is failing.

VISUALIZATION

Visualization is *seeing* in our mind's eye what we have observed in the physical world. Many of us can do this very well. Others not so well. By practice we can all increase our ability to visualize in detail and for periods of extended and dedicated concentration. This ability helps us to see and remember things, people and places, and to evaluate them and *see* them as they really are beneath their surfaces.

PREVISUALIZATION

Previsualization is seeing something that has not yet happened, such as the outcome of a race you're running, or you overcoming an attacker, or seeing yourself digging out step-by-step from a collapsed building or closing a sale with a new customer. If you visualize yourself doing a thing, and really *see* yourself doing it step-by-step, there's a much better chance that the event will happen.

CREATIVE VISUALIZATION

Creative visualization is the art of *seeing* what you cannot see, such as your internal organs. When done properly, and in concert with breathing and energy development, creative visualization can enable us to change our own biochemistry, withstand cold and heat, and heal our own bodies.

VISUALIZATION AND ENERGY

Currently there are many forms of visualization being taught. Some forms seek to assist in reaching personal goals. Others, sometimes taught by medical professionals, focus on healing and pain management. In order to be effective in managing pain and in promoting healing, **visualizations** must be connected to the individual's **body energy,** or chi. Visualizations without that connection will not be effective.

OBJECTS OF ATTENTION

The exercise for each sense to be developed will require an **object of attention,** which is anything to which you direct your attention. We start with one object, but as you progress in your abilities you will use many objects of attention. The idea is to not become overly familiar with one object, but to continually sharpen your abilities to see, hear and perceive by using different objects that require you to start fresh each time. In this way it becomes easy to direct your attention to anything you encounter. As you progress you will find that anything can be an object of attention: a button on your shirt, sunlight on a windowsill, a siren in the distance; and after some progress: a lizard basking on a rock, a stray cat, a person's face in the street, the scent of smoke, the taste of granite-flavored water from a mountain stream, the feel of wind on your skin, the sound of a footfall behind you. The basic exercises separate the senses and focus on enhancing each one separately. Later you will integrate and develop all sensory input.

TUNNELING, TUNNEL VISION AND TARGET FIXATION

Tunneling is excluding all sensory input from your awareness as you direct all of your attention and focus on one thing. **Tunnel vision** is seeing only the object or person in front of you and not using your peripheral vision. **Target fixation** is a process in which your awareness is focused so intently on an object or person that awareness of other obstacles or hazards is diminished. Directing all of your attention to one thing is required in early exercises, and in certain other practices, but must be avoided in nonsecure areas.

YIN AND YANG

In Taoist thought, **yin and yang** is the rhythm of life that ebbs and flows through the universe and permeates all things. This principle is illustrated by the well-known yin and yang symbol, equally divided between dark and light, with each having a portion of the other within itself and each closely connected to the other by a sinuous wave illustrating change. **Yin** is the soft, yielding female life-giving force of the earth. **Yang** is the strong male heat of the sun and the ever-changing heavens. Yin gives way to yang and yang gives way to yin in an eternal cycle. Neither can exist without the other. Balance between the two is the ideal state of being in humans and in the universe.

CENTERING, BREATHING AND ENTERING TAO SPACE

Empty yourself of everything. Let the mind become still.
—Lao Tze

Breathing, centering and entering Tao space are the first steps and foundations of each exercise. Tao space is a survivor's state of mind/body that, once acquired, you will be able to enter at once, while on the move and in high-stress environments. For our primary lessons we'll start in a familiar and comfortable place and take as much time as needed. The format for this lesson is different than those that follow in that you do not need to set an alarm or fixed time for the lesson. The length of the lesson is not determined by time but by the number of breaths and how long it takes you to center and enter Tao space. Some center and slip into Tao space the first time they try. Others require more time, a few much more time.

Others reach Tao space and don't realize they have done so because they are expecting a sudden and dramatic change in their perceptions. Indeed there are, sometimes, dramatic changes in perception. But there is also a subtle level of Tao space that you can find your way to in which you simply seem hyperalert and aware; this is essentially the first level of Tao space. As you progress you will likely find yourself entering deeper levels of Tao space, which will further intensify your experiences. For the purposes of this book, I'll simply refer to Tao space without getting into more detailed and esoteric discussions of different levels.

It doesn't matter if you need one, ten or a hundred repetitions of the basic exercises to be successful. What matters is that you achieve success. Entering Tao space is fundamental to mastery of the following lessons and to developing survivor's mind. Once accomplished, you'll be able to center and enter Tao space easily and quickly and remain as long as you like, perhaps all the time.

There are three exercises in this lesson: sitting, standing and moving. Stay with the first exercise, sitting, until you have mastered it. Once you can center and enter Tao space sitting, go on to standing. After you master standing, go on to moving.

Sitting Exercise

Select a position in which you can sit comfortably for an extended period. Sit with your back straight. It's important to keep your spine as straight as possible to allow the free flow of energy. Visualize a strong, flexible cable attached to the top of your head and holding the weight of your body. As well as aiding in alignment, this also allows your body to spin, turn and move freely in the later exercises involving walking, running and other movement.

Tuck the base of your spine under just a bit. Or think of it as rolling your tailbone under and to the front, or pulling your pelvic bone forward and slightly up by using your lower abdominal muscles, thereby tilting your pelvis and bringing it into proper alignment. This will require some flexion in your lower abdomen. Let your hands rest in your lap.

Close your eyes. For training purposes only, we close our eyes to start the first exercises. Doing so helps us to direct our attention in the beginning. As you acquire expertise, you will not need to close your eyes to shift into Tao space, or to use any of the other skills you will acquire.

With your eyes closed, take in a slow, deep breath and visualize your breath passing through your nose and nasal passages, down through your throat, filling and expanding your lungs and being drawn down into your belly and your tan tien, which you visualize as a balloon the size of a grapefruit just below and behind your navel. This spot is your center of balance, of energy, of your physical and energetic body. Visualizing air and energy being drawn into your tan tien helps to center you, build energy and refine focus. With each breath you take in, see this balloon filling with energy.

Exhale slowly and fully, see your breath rising from your tan tien up through your lungs and throat and out through your mouth. As you breathe out, let the concerns of your day drift away. Allow your mind to become as calm as the surface of a still pond in deep forest. This place of stillness is one you'll become familiar with, a place you'll come back to for all of these exercises and more importantly a state of being you'll create in your mind/body that you'll go to in times of high stress and when you need to act decisively.

Keep your attention on your tan tien, your center. Random thoughts will arise. Allow them to drift away like soap bubbles on the wind. If you wish, you can observe them and name them as they arise: "thinking about work," "thinking about dinner," "thinking about repairing the car," and so on. But do not allow those thoughts to divert your attention from your center. Just note them and let them go.

Take in a second slow, deep breath, expanding your lungs, drawing air and energy down into your tan tien. Allow your muscles and joints to be loose and relaxed; not slack, but softly poised like a cat ready to jump. Keep your attention on your tan tien. Do not force concentration. Allow concentration.

Again, exhale slowly and fully. Your attention will wander to externals: noise in the street, an itch on your arm or nose. When that happens, gently bring your attention back to your center, to stillness. Do not force anything.

Draw in a third deep, slow breath, seeing and feeling air and energy being drawn into your center, your tan tien. Feel the energy and power building in your tan tien so that you could leap up and across the room in a microsecond. You actually will do this in a later lesson. But for this lesson we'll stay in our seats.

As you exhale, feel the energy expanding from your center and suffusing your body. After the third exhalation you will be relaxed, alert, poised and balanced, fully centered and feeling your concentrated power in your tan tien.

Continue breathing and drawing in energy. Now open your eyes. Do not focus on any one thing. Let your eyes be soft and unfocused. See the room around you, the chairs and other furniture, the color of the carpet, the texture of the walls. While keeping attention focused on your ten tien, allow your awareness to expand to take in everything in your environment: the quality of the light streaming through the window, the sounds of passing cars, the drip of water from the kitchen faucet, the fabric of your clothing, the scent of apples in the kitchen. You feel calm, fully aware of your body and your center, your ten tien, and the energy you are drawing in and storing there, and of your surroundings. You are centered and in Tao space.

Remain in this state of centered awareness as long as it is comfortable. Later you will find this state to be restful and can extend your time as much as you want. But for now, for training purposes, limit your time to a few minutes. When you start to tire, take in a slow, deep breath and exhale fully. Stand up and walk around. Think about what you have accomplished. Review step-by-step what you have experienced.

Repeat this exercise each day. It's a simple matter to sit and center for the space of a few breaths when you arise in the morning. Many do this sitting exercise sitting on the side of their bed after awakening. With time and consistent practice you will become centered as a matter of habit.

The next two exercises will be standing and moving while centered and in Tao space.

Standing Exercise

Lao Chung Li, one of the Taoist adepts I studied with in Hong Kong, reminded me every day, "You must do the standing. Without the standing you have no foundation." For the benefits of centering and entering Tao space to be useful in the everyday world and in survival situations, we must be able to center and enter while on our feet and while moving. This lesson focuses on standing; the next will focus on moving.

Stand with your feet at shoulder width, knees slightly bent, feet pointed straight ahead as if you were standing on railroad tracks, and aligned so that your toes are in line with your knees. You should be barefoot or wearing comfortable, thin-soled, flat shoes—no heels. Heels throw your balance forward and make it more difficult to attain correct balance. Shoes, if any, should be wide enough so that your toes can spread and you can flex them individually. Flex your feet and toes as if grasping the floor, or as if you were standing on sand. Remember to keep your spine erect, and visualize a strong, flexible cable attached to the top of your head and holding the weight of your body. Flex the muscles of your lower abdomen and roll your tailbone under and to the front by using your lower abdominal muscles to pull your pelvic bone forward and slightly up, thereby tilting your pelvis and bringing it into proper alignment.

Arms are at your sides, elbows bent with open hands resting by your hips. Visualize your tan tien as a balloon behind and slightly below your navel, and balance your body so that your weight is centered there. Feel your balance so that if you were to move you could move freely in any direction around the balloon. Your eyes are open and soft, unfocused.

Take in a slow, deep breath and visualize breath and energy passing through your nose and nasal passages, down through your throat, filling and expanding your lungs and being drawn down into your belly and your tan tien.

Exhale slowly and fully. Continue breathing, slip into Tao space and relax into this position, maintaining slight tension on your lower abdominal muscles and keeping your tailbone tucked under, and keeping your feet and toes flexed as if you're grasping the floor or a sandy beach. Grasp the floor with your toes. Feel your legs as if they were powerful springs holding you comfortably, strongly. Slightly shift your weight from foot to foot without moving your feet. Raise and lower your weight without moving your feet. Feel how the muscles in your entire body adjust to your shifting weight. Bend your knees a little more and relax deeper into this position. Do not bend your knees any more than is comfortable.

Now, in this comfortable and balanced position expand your vision and awareness to the entire room. Do exactly as you did in the sitting exercise. Do not focus on any one object. Keep your eyes unfocused and soft. Hold this mind/body state and remain in this standing position and state of centered and expanded awareness as long as it is comfortable. When you start to tire, take in a slow, deep breath and exhale fully. Straighten up and walk around or sit. Think about what you have accomplished. Review step-by-step what you have experienced.

If you have the time and energy—these exercises can be very tiring in early lessons, even though to an observer you don't appear to be doing much—add this exercise to the sitting exercise as part of your daily practice. If you're sitting and centering for a few breaths upon arising each day, or at any other time, simply rise to a standing position and do the standing exercise for the space of a few breaths, or longer if you prefer and as your schedule allows.

Moving Exercise

Begin by taking the standing position you have practiced. Do not skip any of the steps. Breathe in deeply, bringing air and energy to your tan tien. Balance yourself as before and shift your weight from side to side and up and down without moving your feet.

Remember while moving to keep your spine erect. Visualize a strong, flexible cable attached to the top of your head and holding the weight of your body. Maintain slight tension in your lower abdominal muscles and keep your tailbone tucked or rolled under and to the front and your pelvic bone pushed forward and slightly up, thereby tilting your pelvis and bringing it into proper alignment.

When you have fully settled into Tao space, centered and with expanded awareness, take a step forward. Keep your head level. Do not bob up and down. Do not straighten your knees. Lift one foot and slowly move it forward. Keep all your weight on your rear foot. Do not strike your heel or land on it hard. Place your leading foot down softly, carefully and lightly, shifting your weight forward and rolling from heel to toes, keeping your feet and toes strong and flexed as if grasping the floor with your toes, or as if you were walking on sand.

If your balance is correct you will be able to freeze your motion at any point—while standing on either or both feet and without losing your balance.

Grasping the floor with the toes of your leading foot, shift your weight forward, moving so that your knee is over your foot. Move slowly and carefully, as if you were walking on ice. Bring your rear foot forward, past the front foot, placing what is now your leading foot down softly, lightly and rolling from heel to toes.

Walk around your house like this for as long as it's comfortable, continuing to breathe into your tan tien. While doing so, use the same method—shifting weight slowly, grasping the floor with your toes, etc.—and step sideways and at various angles. Turn and walk in a circle to your left, then to your right. Walk backwards. Move around furniture, seeing all that you can see as you move around. Stay centered and visualize your body as moving around your tan tien.

When you start to tire, take in a slow, deep breath and exhale fully. Straighten up to ease your leg muscles, sit down and rest. Think about what you have accomplished. Review step-by-step what you have experienced.

Add the moving exercise to each day's practice of sitting and standing. Repeat the entire lesson—sitting, standing and moving—each day. Once the basics are mastered, it's a simple matter to sit and center for the space of a few breaths when you arise in the morning, and then flow from sitting to standing, and from standing to moving. The entire process should take no more than a minute or so. With time, you'll do it in seconds. Do this each morning, holding your focus as you go to the bathroom, and you'll not slip and fall in the shower—and you'll be centered and ready for your day.

Little by little, over a couple of weeks or so, shorten the process so that you can center and enter Tao space in two breaths. Then one breath. You will find that with practice you can easily put yourself into centered Tao space with only one breath, and in time with a partial breath, or none. You will be able to do so while walking, running or driving.

Follow this practice and make it part of your daily routine. Check your center from time to time. If you are not centered, center. Do it consciously more than once a day, whenever you rise from any chair, when standing, walking, running, playing basketball or whatever other exercise you do, and with time you will instinctively move fully balanced and centered and be able to instantly enter Tao space.

FOCUSED ATTENTION, SENSORY INPUT AND VISUALIZATION

SIGHT AND SEEING

A Sherpa guide once said of the people who come to Nepal to see the Himalayas and Mount Everest, and to find the magic that so many have found in these storied mountains, "Many people come, looking, looking. But no one *sees*." By this he meant that visitors from the West looked only at surfaces and failed to see deeply into what was in front of them, and therefore did not truly *see* the essence of the mountains or their glory and majesty, nor did they find what they sought.

Obviously sight and seeing are not always the same thing. *Seeing* is sometimes used to mean the sum of all senses. But in this exercise we're using it in the sense of sight. For most of us sight is our primary sense, the one we rely on for most of our information. But few of us see much of what there is to see around us each day.

Your first goal is to truly see one thing, to see it clearly and deeply, to see it in detail and to see it whole. Each detail tells you about the thing you're observing, its purpose and beginnings. Then you'll expand your vision and see many things—in effect, as if you were looking through a camera lens and going from a narrow telephoto view to a wide-angle view. Then you'll shift back and forth from wide-angle to telephoto.

Aside from other benefits and uses, mastering this way of seeing will help you to scan a crowd and pick out a person of interest—a lost child or a person with ill intent; to scan woods and fields and pick out animals; to find the one edible plant in a jungle.

NARROW FOCUS

Start by selecting a visual object of attention. When teaching I often have my students use a flower, because they are pleasant to look at and possess great detail. I also frequently use a rock, because you can find one almost anyplace and they also have much detail.

The following instructions provide details for a daisy—a common flower—and a rock. If you do not have either, substitute in the instructions details of whatever object you have selected: the weave of your shirt, the texture of a concrete wall, a steel bar, a button, the cover of this book.

For the first exercise, set an alarm for seven minutes, then shorten the duration as you progress to shorter periods. Setting an alarm removes schedule anxieties. You won't be wondering if your time is up and can relax and focus on the exercise. Find a quiet place where outside distractions do not intrude, and a time when you won't be disturbed. You do not have to be on a secluded mountaintop. The front seat of your parked car, your bedroom or a corner of your yard will do.

If you are interrupted, return to the exercise when you are able. If outside noise or other distractions intrude, simply regard them as part of your practice. While primary lessons are easiest to learn in a distraction-free place, you'll later be doing all these things in high-stress environments. If you cannot find a quiet spot, simply do the exercises wherever you happen to be, so long as you're not in a place where directing your attention to one object would endanger you or anyone else. Doing these exercises while driving is *not* a good idea. You knew that, right?

Seven-Minute Exercise

Select a position in which you can sit comfortably for an extended time. Place your object of attention where you can see it from where you will be sitting without bending your neck or straining in any way. As in the previous exercise on centering, sit with your back straight. Let your hands rest in your lap.

Close your eyes. For training purposes only, we close our eyes to start the beginning exercises. Doing so helps us to direct our attention in the beginning. As you acquire skill, you will not need to close your eyes to shift into directed attention mode. You will be able to do so with eyes open and while on the run.

With your eyes closed, take in a slow, deep breath. See, that is visualize, your breath passing through your nose and nasal passages, down through your throat, filling your lungs and being drawn down into your belly and your tan tien, just below and behind your navel. Remember, this spot is your center of balance, of energy, of your physical and energetic body. As you exhale, see your breath rising from your tan tien up through your lungs and throat and out through your mouth. Each breath should be slow and steady and deep.

Take three deep, slow breaths. As you breathe out, let the concerns of your day drift away. Allow your mind to become as calm as the surface of a still pond in deep forest. After the third exhalation you will be centered and in Tao space. Open your eyes, focus your vision and direct all of your attention at your object of attention.

A Daisy as Your Object of Attention

Observe your daisy closely. Is the stem rigid or flexible, dark green or light? See how the petals are attached to the base of the flower. See the grooves in each petal. Are the petals white or off-white? See deep into the center of the flower. Is it golden or yellow? How do you think it would feel to stroke the petals with your finger and touch its center? If you brought the daisy to your nose would it have a scent? Sink your attention deep into the flower. Think about how the flower would look if you were so small you could sit inside of it.

As thoughts and distractions intrude—what you need to do at work tomorrow, what's for dinner, a horn honking in the street, your nose itching—let those distractions and thoughts drift away, like bubbles in a stream. When your attention wanders, bring it back to your daisy. Keep all your attention on your daisy. Observe finer and finer details: how the ends of the petals are shaped, how they taper, where they attach to the center, the tiny pistils poking up in the center.

What do these details tell you about your flower? Where did it come from? How did it develop? What is its purpose? Does it face towards the sun, or grow in the shade? See this flower as you've never before seen any flower. See its daisyness.

If you are totally focused and breathing correctly, you will see the essence of this flower, and have taken further steps into Tao space. Later you'll find that these kinds of directed attention questions will reveal much to you about other things, and about people.

Continue to direct all of your attention at your flower until your alarm rings. Turn off your alarm, get up and walk around.

Visualization Exercise

Return to where you were sitting and set your alarm for one minute. Once again take in and let out three deep breaths, being fully focused and bringing the air into and up from your tan tien, and enter Tao space.

With your eyes closed, see your flower with your mind's eye. Visualize your daisy as you have observed it. Mentally recreate its image to the finest detail. Allow yourself the full minute for visualization. When your vision of the flower is complete, open your eyes and see how close the physical flower is to your visualization. Don't be discouraged if it's not a close match. Simply repeat the exercise until your mental picture is close enough to allow you to pick your flower out of a bouquet of similar flowers.

A Rock as Your Object of Attention

Follow all instructions for breathing and centering as above for the daisy. After the third exhalation, open your eyes and focus your vision and all of your attention on your object of attention.

Observe it closely. What color is your rock? Is it smooth or rough; round, egg-shaped or irregular? Does it have scrapes and scars? How did it get them? How much does it weigh? See deep into your rock. Can you see it being formed by the forces of the earth? How would it feel to the touch? Imagine if you were small enough to sit on top of your rock; how would it feel under you?

As thoughts and distractions intrude—what you need to do at work tomorrow, what's for dinner, a horn honking in the street, your nose itching—let those distractions and thoughts drift away, like bubbles in a stream. When your attention wanders, bring it back to your rock. Keep all your attention on your rock. Observe finer and finer details.

What do these details tell you about your rock? Where did it come from? How did it develop? Was it pushed up from under the earth, or did it fall from a mountain? What is its purpose? Does it have any uses? See this rock as you've never before seen any rock.

Continue to direct all of your attention at your rock until your alarm rings. Turn off your alarm, get up and walk around.

Visualization Exercise

Return to where you were sitting, set your alarm for one minute and once again take in and let out three fully focused deep breaths, bringing air and energy into your tan tien. Close your eyes and see your rock with your mind's eye. Visualize the rock as you have observed it. Mentally recreate its image to the finest detail. Allow yourself a full minute for visualization. When your vision of the rock is complete, open your eyes and see how close the physical rock is to your visualization. Don't be discouraged if it's not a close match. Simply repeat the exercise until your mental picture is close enough to allow you to pick your rock out of a pile of similar rocks.

When you have repeated this exercise three times and made good progress, stop and clear your mind, get up, walk around. Then review how well you've done. If you choose, you can check your progress by writing down details of your visualization and how it differs from the actual object.

After resting, or perhaps at another time depending on your schedule and alertness, go on to the three-minute exercise. Even though you appear to be sitting and doing nothing, this training can be quite tiring. Allow yourself enough rest time before going to the next exercise.

Three-Minute Exercise

The only difference between the three-minute and the seven-minute exercise is duration. However, this is a significant difference. Now you will need to strengthen and intensify your concentration. Being well centered and in Tao space is key to success. Any distraction will hamper your progress.

Select a new object of attention. Set your alarm and do the three-minute exercise three times, visualizing after each exercise and following the same instructions as for the seven-minute exercise.

One-Minute Exercise

By shortening the duration for each exercise step-by-step, we learn to quickly see what previously has required periods of time that might not be available in a crisis. The one-minute exercise should be a relatively easy transition from the three-minute exercise. Set your alarm and do the one-minute exercise three times, visualizing after each exercise and following the same instructions as for the previous exercises.

Ten-Second Exercise

Seeing as much in ten seconds as you have been able to see in one minute requires close concentration, firm centering and unwavering directed attention. It will also require a different kind of concentration. To master this step you will need to "see quickly," and to "take your time in a hurry." This is something difficult if not impossible to describe. The only way to experience it is to do it.

One-Breath Exercise

At this point we're also going to move ahead and get into Tao space with only one breath, as you did in the first exercises. Start with a new object of concentration and follow the previous instructions exactly, but focus your attention into one breath. Building on the skills acquired in previous exercises, some make this jump fairly easily. Others will find the challenge difficult.

Take in one long, slow, deep breath and see air and energy passing through your nose and nasal passages, down through your throat, filling your lungs and being drawn down into your tan tien. Remember, this spot is your center of balance, of energy, of your physical and energetic body. As you exhale, see your breath rising from your tan tien up through your lungs and throat and out through your mouth. This breath should be slow, steady, deep and centering.

Controlling your breath and centering is a key point in all of these exercises. Allowing your breath to get away from you can interfere with your concentration and allow your attention to become scattered.

If, after three repetitions of the exercise, you find that you cannot acquire enough information and a firm enough image of your object of attention to clearly visualize it within ten seconds, allow yourself twenty seconds and start again. However, do not allow yourself to do more than three repetitions at the twenty-second level, as it will hinder your progress. If you do not master the ten-second exercise within three to nine repetitions, take a break and come back to it the next day. Make sure you have the ten-second interval firmly mastered before taking the next important step.

One-Second Exercise

To see as much in one second as you have been able to do in ten times the amount of time is something many find difficult. Some students get stuck at this level for many more than three repetitions of the exercise. Others breeze through it, finding it as easy, perhaps easier, to see an object as fully in this short time as they did during the longer intervals.

In either case, it's time to vary the process. Select and place your object of attention, choose a place to sit and equip yourself with a flashlight. Take your seat and, if you're inside, turn off the room lights. Wherever you've chosen to sit, it should be dark enough so that you cannot clearly see your object of attention without a light.

As before, breathe in and out one time, slowly and deeply, down into your tan tien. Then, centered and with your attention firmly directed at your object, switch *on the flashlight for what you judge to be one second and quickly switch it off.*

At first it might seem that a one-second flash of light is too brief to capture the image of your object and allow you to visualize it. Persevere. Soon enough you'll find that a full second is a very long time. You may master this in only three repetitions. Many do, while others require more than three repetitions.

It's likely that you will be unable to see as much detail in one second as you did in seven minutes or three minutes, or even ten seconds. That's normal. What matters most is that you learn to capture the high points and essential details to allow accurate visualization. This is a critical skill, one that should be mastered before moving on. A day might come when you only have a flash of light to determine whether the person coming towards you is a friend or foe.

When you have mastered the one-second exercise, continue to shorten the time to split seconds. To accurately measure intervals this short requires specialized equipment. For our purposes such equipment is not needed. Just shorten the time your flashlight illuminates your object of attention. You will learn how much you can see in a split second and will acquire confidence as you progress.

As you go about your daily life, make it a habit to center with one breath and quickly look at an object and then look away. If you're at your desk or another place where it's safe to do so, close your eyes and visualize the object. With time, this skill, like the others, will become automatic.

You may find that for you one of the primary values of this kind of seeing is the enhanced ability to see individual objects in traffic, and to evaluate their motion and determine whether they are a hazard to themselves or to you. For those who are in high-threat zones, the benefits are obvious.

WIDE FOCUS

Many years ago I was traveling in rural Guatemala with a friend, Mike, a very competent former Special Forces soldier. We stopped at a small *posada,* a country hotel, for the night. The *posada's* facilities were basic: bathroom down the hall, no heat or air conditioning. We stopped at the door to our room for a moment to survey the muddy courtyard and a cow tethered to a tree. Mike unlocked the door and entered the room. As I picked up my rucksack I heard a terrified scream from inside the room. I looked in just in time to see a fighting rooster, spurs on point, flying across the room at Mike. The rooster hit Mike, who was wearing shorts, and with his razor sharp spurs furiously slashed Mike's legs and groin area.

I grabbed Mike around the chest and pulled him backwards away from the rooster and out of the room, which the rooster evidently considered his territory, and slammed the door shut. The owner came to see what the ruckus was about and secured the rooster, thereby saving the critter from Mike's wrath. Fortunately Mike's shorts were made of sturdy fabric. Some first aid and a bottle of mescal took care of the wounds. Mike said, "That sucker was sitting right in the middle of the room and I didn't see him till he was in the air and coming at me. I didn't know what the hell he was."

For this exercise, select a room and a spot in the room where you can sit comfortably and have a good view of the room. It's better to start with an unfamiliar room, in that you will probably already have a pretty good image in your mind of a more familiar room. It's best to use a different room for each exercise, but if you cannot use different rooms, rearrange some of the objects in your room before each exercise.

During this exercise hold your head in one position. Do not turn to see more. You want to see as much as you can see within your field of vision and learn to better use your peripheral vision. Later you will turn your head to shift your field of vision. But first we need to learn to see all there is to see in front of us.

Seven-Minute Exercise

As in the narrow focus exercise, set your alarm for seven minutes. Close your eyes and take one slow, deep breath to center and enter Tao space. Open your eyes and hold them steady, in a fixed gaze looking straight ahead. Do not scan from side to side or up and down. Remember, one of the purposes of this exercise is to develop your peripheral vision, which is best done this way. See and note all you can see within your fixed field of vision. Blink as needed.

Do not focus on any single object. In this exercise we are not concerned with fine detail of a particular thing. What we want is an overall picture that includes all the objects—and people, if any—in the room. Surprisingly, some students have done this exercise and failed to notice a person sitting in the room within their field of vision.

See everything in your field of vision: tables, chairs, the carpet, the color of the wall, an overhead light, doors and windows, objects sitting on furniture, glasses, plates, bottles, books. Think about the objects and the room. That half-full glass sitting on the table—whose is it? Is the light harsh, or soft and pleasing? Why is the table placed where it is? Is there an exit within your field of vision?

Although not part of this exercise, you should, as a matter of course, learn the locations of all exits, doors and windows of any room you enter. More on that later.

By now you will be familiar with directed attention and the distractions that arise. You will be adept at allowing irrelevant thoughts and minor bodily distractions to drift away like bubbles in a stream. Your concentration will have improved, but still it will waver. This is normal. Continue to breathe easily and deeply into your center, and direct your full attention to the room in front of you.

If it's a familiar room, see it as you've never before seen it. If an unfamiliar room, see it as if it will become your room and you must know it as well as your own room. See everything—miss nothing. Identify every object in your field of vision. Direct your attention to seeing all there is to see in your field of vision. Concentrate as if your life or well-being depended on it, as it might one day if you're ever unfortunate enough to enter a room where there's an improvised explosive device, or a fierce rooster.

Continue to direct all of your attention into your room until your alarm rings. Turn off your alarm, get up and walk around.

Visualization Exercise

Return to your chair, set your alarm for one minute and once again take in and let out one deep breath, fully focused and bringing the air into and up from your center.

Close your eyes and see the room with your mind's eye. Visualize the room as you have observed it. Mentally recreate its image to the finest detail. Allow yourself a full minute for visualization. When your vision of the room is complete, open your eyes and see how close the physical room is to your visualization. Don't be discouraged if it's not a close match. Repeat the exercise until your mental picture approaches the accuracy of a photograph of the room.

As in the narrow focus exercise, repeat the seven-minute exercise and the visualizations three times.

Three-Minute Exercise

Go to another room, or rearrange your room, and proceed as before. Do not leave out any steps: set a three-minute alarm, select a comfortable place to sit, close your eyes, breathe in and out once and center. Remember, closing your eyes is at this point a training aid. In actual use you will not need to close your eyes to enter a concentrated directed attention mode. Each time, after seeing the room, visualize it. Repeat three times.

One-Minute Exercise

Go to another room, or rearrange your room, and proceed as before. Do not leave out any steps: set a one-minute alarm, select a comfortable place to sit, close your eyes, breathe in and out slowly one time and become centered. Each time, after seeing the room, visualize it. Repeat three times.

Ten-Second Exercise

Having acquired the skill required to see all that's in front of your fixed field of vision in one minute, it's now time to change the exercise and shorten the time.

Stand outside a room you have not yet used for this exercise, or one you have rearranged, with the door closed. Set a ten-second alarm. Take a deep breath to center and enter Tao space, and prepare to direct your attention to the room you're about to see. Quickly open the door and look inside with a fixed field of view for ten seconds. When the alarm sounds, close the door.

Stay in place, close your eyes and visualize the room in ten seconds. Can you *see* in your mind's eye everything that was in your field of vision?

Repeat three times.

One-Second Exercise

As with the narrow focus exercise, this one-second exercise requires total concentrated directed attention. Remember, do not scan; scanning comes next. For this exercise keep your field of vision constant and see everything within it.

Having acquired the experience of seeing one object of attention in one second, you know it's possible to see everything in front of you in one second. Remember, see everything but do not focus tightly on one object; we'll soon get to that exercise.

Start with a new room, or rearrange your room. Do everything as before. Imagine a flash photo of the room. That's the effect you seek. Visualize after each exercise.

Repeat three times.

SCANNING

We commonly use our vision to scan. We scan traffic to assess conditions, watch for possible unsafe conditions and keep our own car in a safe position. Since we have established basic skills with the previous exercises, and because we are already familiar with scanning, we will now shorten the duration of the exercises and start with a one-minute exercise, go to ten seconds, then to one second. Given these shorter time periods, your attention will need to be fully directed and concentrated. Although familiar with scanning, most people skip over things right in front of them—sometimes important things.

While scanning, you'll see many things you did not see when you limited your vision to a fixed field. But by now you've most likely used all the rooms in your house and become familiar with them to the extent that the next exercises would be less effective due to overfamiliarity. To give yourself a fresh perspective, rearrange all the furniture and various objects in the room where you'll be working before you begin.

One-Minute Exercise

As before, select a room and a comfortable place to sit, set a one-minute alarm, close your eyes, breathe in and out slowly once, center and enter Tao space. Remember, closing your eyes is at this point a training aid. In actual use you will not need to close your eyes to enter a concentrated directed attention mode or Tao space. Entering Tao space will become automatic and happen in a split second if you persevere with the exercises.

When you open your eyes, see what is within your field of vision then quickly scan the entire room side to side, top to bottom—including the ceiling. As you scan, be sure to use your full field of vision, including your peripheral vision, as you have done previously. Do not allow your vision to tunnel or focus on one object. As a training aid, one of my instructors once placed a television tuned to MTV in our training room and told us to come in. He had also placed an enormous, bright red Chinese firework, a Roman candle, with the fuse burning on a table. No one noticed the Roman candle, until the firework went off. Then they did.

For this exercise, scan—do not focus. See everything in the room, large and small objects, the carpet and anything on it, the ceiling, windows and curtains. Scan the entire room and see as much detail as you possibly can. Imagine that you're scanning for a lost kitten or a deadly spider, but do not yet focus on one item.

Visualization Exercise

Now close your eyes and visualize the entire room. Can you create in your mind's eye the room and all its details? Most likely you've come pretty close. Few can re-create a room in its totality, but you should be able to see and visualize most, if not all, of the objects in the room, and in some detail: the weave of the carpet, the bowl of fruit, the cup filled with coffee, or was it tea?

Repeat three times using a different room each time if possible. If you cannot use different rooms, rearrange objects in the room before each exercise.

Ten-Second Exercise

By now you've developed your ability to direct your attention in a concentrated manner and quickly. Also, you have probably found that since it's something you're more familiar with, you've quickly acquired accurate scanning ability. Making the jump to a ten-second scan should go smoothly.

For this exercise we'll again stand outside a room with the door closed. Use a room you have not yet used for this exercise, or one you or a friend has rearranged. Set a ten-second alarm. Take a deep breath, center and prepare to direct your attention to the room you're about to see. Quickly open the door and scan the entire room for ten seconds. When the alarm sounds, close the door.

Stay in place, close your eyes and visualize the room. Can you see in your mind's eye everything in the room? Was there a kitten under a table or a spider on the ceiling?

Repeat three times.

One-Second Exercise

For many students, having built on the previous training, the jump to a one-second scan is easy. Consider that you use visual scanning almost constantly when out and about. The primary difference between that sort of scanning and what we're learning to do in these exercises is that here we're learning to see more.

Follow the instructions for the ten-second scan, but only open the door for one second. Visualize after each exercise. You will probably find that you can visualize the room with about the same amount of detail that you could when you had ten seconds. Was there a rooster in the room?

Repeat three times.

SCANNING AND SHIFTING FOCUS

Now we shift back and forth from scanning to close focus. This is the kind of vision you would use, and possibly *have* used, when, for example, you try to locate a snake in the yard that has alarmed your child. This is the kind of vision that is absolutely critical to survival in certain situations. Some rooms have things more dangerous than roosters in them, and some of the snakes that live in yards are rattlesnakes.

Unfortunately, most people do not use this natural ability as well as they could. I have seen an entire group of untrained people fail to spot a tear gas grenade with the pin pulled sitting in plain sight in the middle of a table. They only noticed it after the fuse popped and gas started coming out—too late if it had been a fragmentation grenade, and maybe too late if it had been a rattlesnake. Developing this natural ability, scanning and focusing, is as critical to the survivor as developing strength is to an Olympic weight lifter. If you cannot spot a hazard, you cannot avoid or neutralize it.

You will need a friend's assistance for these exercises. Select a familiar room. Have a friend add one object to the room. Ask your friend to select an object of reasonable size (you do not want to begin by trying to find a postage stamp under a chair). They should not tell you what the object is, and should place it where it can be seen from the door (discourage your friend from having some fun by placing a spoon in a drawer or the like).

Ten-Second Exercise

Stand outside the room with the door closed where your friend has placed one object that was not previously in the room. Set a ten-second alarm. Take one deep breath, center, enter Tao space and prepare to direct your attention to the room you're about to see. Quickly open the door and scan the entire room for ten seconds. When the alarm sounds, close the door.

Did you see the object your friend placed? If not, try again. Repeat until you either see the object or must ask where and what it is. If you were successful, have your friend change the object.

Repeat three times with a new object each time.

One-Second Exercise

Shorten the duration of the exercise to one second, again with a different object. By now you should be quickly spotting the new object. If so, repeat three times; if not, go back to the previous exercise and work your way through the process again. Remember, one breath and center before each exercise.

To further sharpen your abilities, have your friend place smaller objects in less obvious places each time; possibly hang a small balloon from the ceiling, or tape a banana to a chair leg.

NIGHT VISION

Unless you have a vitamin deficiency or genetic hindrance, you can see in the dark better than you might think you can. Unless you are in a totally dark room that is sealed off from all light, or deep in a cave, there is almost always some ambient light available. Your eyes have evolved over millennia to take advantage of available light. Electric light, with its constant availability and our use of it, has transformed civilization and eased our lives in innumerable ways. But with the constant use of artificial light, and our dependence on it, most of us have never tried to make use of the night-vision abilities we have. Even backpackers and wilderness campers rarely make use of the night vision available to them, relying instead on flashlights and lanterns rather than natural ability. Humans cannot see as well in the dark as a cat, but a very simple shift in the use of your eyes will enable you to see quite well in the dark—much better than you might think.

Exercise 1

Start by turning off all the lights in your house. Draw the curtains or blinds and do whatever you can to block light from outside. Allow about ten minutes for your eyes to adjust to reduced light. Sit comfortably, breathe, focus, center and slip into Tao space. Close your eyes tightly for ten seconds. Open your eyes and let them go soft, slightly out of focus.

The experience you gained in the wide focus lesson that improved your peripheral vision will also help with night vision. Your eyes are more sensitive to light and contrast at their edges. Scan the room side to side, up and down. Do not stare directly at anything. Use your peripheral vision to look for contrast and shadows to define objects. Little by little the room and the objects will be revealed to your night vision.

After another ten minutes, stand up into your centered position. Step forward, using the centered and balanced walk you have learned, and walk slowly around the room. Scan from side to side and up and down as you walk. Remember to rely on your peripheral vision. If it's so dark you are unsure about the location of all objects, extend one hand in front of yourself and move it slowly from side to side, as if feeling for cobwebs.

Once you are confident about moving around the room, move on to the other rooms. Taking your time and moving slowly, go through your entire house. If you do stumble into something, simply stop, determine what the object is and move around it.

Guard against a loss of all your night vision by being prepared to close one eye if someone should turn on a light. By closing one eye you retain your night vision in that eye until the light source is extinguished.

Exercise 2

After you're confident about moving around in your home with no lights, go outside at night and try it in your yard. If you're in a rural area on a clear night, the stars and moon—especially a full moon—will provide enough light for you to see shapes of objects and shadows. If you're in a city, where the city lights blot out the stars and moon, the glow of those lights will do as well.

Do not go wandering around in the mountains at night and risk falling off a cliff. Trained personnel move slowly—very, very slowly—at night and in unfamiliar territory, and see almost as much with "perception"—which we'll practice later—as with their eyes.

Wearing sunglasses during sunny days improves night vision by as much as 50 percent.

HEARING

Everyone knows that blind people's hearing is superior to that of sighted people due to the compensating sharpening of their hearing. Have you ever tried being blind for a while?

Exercise 1

For this first exercise, place a bowl in your kitchen sink under the tap and turn on the water so that it slowly drips into the bowl. Sit where you can hear the dripping water. Tie a handkerchief or scarf around your eyes. Sit comfortably, breathe, focus, center and slip into Tao space. Stay with these exercises for at least seven minutes. Longer is better.

Direct your attention to the sound of water drops falling into the bowl. At first the drops will strike the bottom of the bowl and make a distinctive sound. Note how the sound changes as the bowl fills and the drops strike water, and then changes again as the bowl overflows.

Exercise 2

Repeat the exercise with wind chimes or bells, or a recording of bells or wind chimes. Focusing on a single sound and the subtle differences in the sound of water dripping, bells or wind chimes will help to sensitize and develop your sense of sound and your ability to pick out tiny variations in the sounds of your daily life, which is partially why temple bells are often used to focus attention.

For these initial exercises stay with simple sounds. Music comes with complications. Later, it would be a good exercise to listen—really listen—to various kinds of music and reflect on how different kinds make you feel. I see commuters on city streets with their car windows open listening to headbanger or hip-hop or hard rock music and getting red-faced and angry when traffic stalls. Some of them pound on their dashboards or scream out the window at other drivers. Acting out road rage is only a small step away for these people. Is it only traffic that creates these emotions, or does the music contribute? What if they were listening to a Brahms waltz? Would the waltz change their experience and emotions?

Follow the sound with all your attention. Get into the sound and flow with it. Turn off the recording or silence the dripping water or bells or wind chimes and recreate the sound in your mind. See if you can get into the sound, and flow with it as you did when you were hearing the actual sound.

Exercise 3

Now, standing and with a scarf or handkerchief wrapped around your eyes, breathe, center, slip into Tao space, then tap the floor or furniture with a stick or cane. Direct your attention to the sound of the tapping and the echoes it makes. Listen and sense the dimensions of the room. Slowly walk through your house, tapping as you go. How well can you find your way? Imagine if you lost your sight, say in a dust storm while hiking in the desert. Could you find your way back to your car?

Exercise 4

Now, as with vision, we'll go wide and hear everything we can hear, then pick out individual sounds. Sit comfortably in your home with the windows open. Breathe, center and enter Tao space. Open your awareness to all the sounds around you and those far away. The hum of the refrigerator compressor, hammers hitting nails at the construction site on the next block, tires on asphalt, the fluttering of a bird's wings, honeybees buzzing. Is that faucet still dripping?

As you hear all the things there are to hear in your environment, direct your attention to various individual sounds. Can you hear rhythms in that compressor's cycle? How many bees are buzzing, or is that buzz coming from a rattlesnake under the rosebush? Is there a car stopping in front of your house? Can you hear a cat walking on a fence?

Make directed listening part of your daily routine. The heightened sensitivity you've acquired could save you from injury, or worse. Suppose you're walking on a sidewalk in your neighborhood, and through the sounds of traffic from the nearby busy street you hear the scrape of a dog's nails on concrete as your neighbor's unruly pit bull rushes at you from behind. Suppose you're awakened from sleep by the sound of a window being slowly pried open in your living room. In either instance, rather than being caught unaware, you'll have time to react due to your sensitivity to sound. You might also hear faint music far away and follow it to its source and find yourself in the middle of a free concert in a park, with people smiling and laughing and having a good time, and one of them might hand you a cold drink and invite you to join the party.

SMELLING

A young woman I once knew, Mary, saved her life and those of her husband and three-year-old son, by her sense of smell, quick reactions and centered decision-making in the face of danger. She and her son were asleep late at night in winter. An electric wire shorted out under the carpet in the living room and the carpet caught fire. The scent of smoke awakened the young mother. She immediately leapt from bed, ran to the living room and saw the room aflame, the fire spreading and her husband asleep on the couch where he had been working on his laptop. Mary couldn't awaken her husband and realized he had been overcome by smoke. Recognizing that it was too late to stop the fire, she decided to get her husband and son out of the house. Her husband was much larger than she; no way could she pick him up. But he was close to the fire and in the most danger. She dragged him by his arms to the front hallway and left him there, then ran to her son's room, grabbed him in her arms and carried him to the lawn, where she left him while dragging her husband's unconscious body out of the house, down the steps and into the yard. Mary did not pause and try to put out an already raging fire or call the fire department. She reacted at once to her senses, and without hesitation acted on her best instincts and survived. The fire department came after Mary called them from a neighbor's house. The paramedics revived her husband. Mary, her husband and son watched the firefighter's efforts to save their house while wrapped in blankets the neighbors had given them. Everything in the house was destroyed, but Mary and her family had their lives.

Exercise 1

As we did in previous exercises, we start with one scent. Select a stick of incense and set it alight in a holder or over a bowl. Yes, one of the reasons they use incense in temples is to focus the sense of smell. To aid in directing your attention to your sense of smell, wrap a scarf or handkerchief around your eyes, and put cotton balls or earplugs in your ears. Sit comfortably, breathe, center and enter Tao space. By now you're accustomed to these exercises and able to set your own periods of duration, but do try to stay with the seven-minute period. It is the most effective.

As you continue to breathe slowly and deeply, direct your attention to the scent of the incense. Sight and sound do not at this moment exist for you. There is only the wafting scent. What is it—lavender, jasmine, patchouli? Does the scent arouse any feelings? Can you follow the scent, drifting along with it back to its source? Will you be able to recognize this scent again, even if you get only a faint whiff of it?

Change the incense to another scent and repeat. Place a single rose nearby and repeat.

Exercise 2

To go wide and selective, go outside and find a comfortable place to sit. This time simply close your eyes and put your hands over your ears. Breathe, center and enter Tao space. Direct your attention to your sense of smell and expand it to encompass all around you: the new mown grass, the scent of your wooden fence under the heat of the sun, the acrid smell of rotting orange peels from your garbage can. Pick out one scent from all others and follow it to its source.

Do the same exercise with your eyes and ears open. Switch from wide- to narrow-focused smell as you walk around your neighborhood. As with the other exercises, make them part of your day. With time, all your senses become more sensitive.

The sense of smell is much underrated in our culture. Mostly we try to suppress it. But scent can save your life, as it did those of Mary and her family. If you were to go to a shooting range and the fellow next to you on the firing line smelled like a brewery, you might want to leave the facility. A young couple I once knew escaped being kidnapped from a four-star hotel in Mexico City because the young woman smelled cigarette smoke as her husband turned the key to the door to their nonsmoking hotel room. Having been alerted to this danger by the embassy, she grabbed her husband's arm and they instantly stepped backwards, slammed the door shut and ran for the exit. They reached the stairwell, ran down three flights of stairs and into the crowded lobby before the would-be kidnappers could catch them.

Scent, whether actual or remembered, is also a powerful memory trigger, and can help you to recall details of past events. When I think back to a training hall in Hong Kong, I smell peanut oil and vegetables cooking in the restaurant downstairs and the whole scene comes into focus. The smell of wet earth can take me back to a house in Bali next to a rice paddy, and then I remember the roosters crowing at first light and the feel of cool tile underfoot.

TOUCH AND SKIN SENSE

Can you feel a mosquito land on your neck and swat it before it gives you an itchy bite, and maybe malaria? Do you feel that black widow spider walking up your leg as you sit in your lawn chair reading? Can you feel air currents on your back from a silently opened door? Fingertips to toes, your skin has nerve endings. Our skin is the largest organ of our bodies and not just a covering to hold the package together. In addition to its other functions, skin is a *sense* organ.

Exercise

For this exercise it's best to go outside in a secure location, such as your yard. Wear only shorts. This is a tough one in winter. If it's snowing, either wait for spring or do this exercise inside until you've mastered all the lessons in this book, including those on body temperature control.

Use a scarf to obstruct vision and earplugs to block sound. Use a clip or plugs to block your now sensitized sense of smell and breathe through your mouth for the duration of this exercise. Seven minutes to start is best. Sit, breathe through your mouth slowly and deeply, center and enter Tao space.

Whether inside or outside, direct your attention to the surface of your skin. Start with your face, then direct your attention down over your neck, your shoulders, down your arms to your elbows, forearms, hands and fingertips, down your torso and over your thighs, knees, shins and calves to your feet and then toes. Visualize the skin over your entire body as having nerve endings extending slightly, microscopically, from each pore. Take enough time with this step to see and feel those nerve endings.

Next, from the skin with its nerve endings over your entire body, extend your awareness. Feel air currents, heat or cold, vibrations from footsteps, the texture of the chair under your thighs and on your back. Extend further to feel all the rooms in your house, or to the boundaries of your yard. This is familiar territory to you. You know what is in this space. But now, with all other senses blocked and with your skin sensitized, further expand your awareness. Reach out and feel what is there, especially anything moving. Can you feel a possum walking through the weeds or a mouse scampering under the roof?

In some ways this sense is the most difficult to develop. We wear clothing all the time and for the most part do not think of our skin as a sense organ. But persevere and you'll find new sensitivities you had not imagined.

After the sitting exercise, do some walking exercises—although this time *not* with your other senses blocked. When you're next at the beach or a swimming pool, direct your attention to your skin rather than at the girl or guy sunbathing in the skimpy swimsuit—at least for a minute or so. Feel the sun on your skin, sand underfoot, water as it passes over you.

Walk away from your campfire and wander around the woods, desert or mountains at night in only moccasins or slippers and shorts. Naked would be better, but you might stub your toe or alarm the wildlife. Even with the use of your night sight, sensitized hearing and smell, you'll develop sensors on your skin to feel air currents, the slightest touch of a leaf falling, weeds brushing your ankles.

I've spent time with native hunters in Asia who wear nothing but a covering for their private parts. They tell me they can feel on their skin the passing of a snake, the movements of a jungle cat, the vibrations of leaves settling to earth. I believe them. I can't do what they can do, but I can feel those pesky mosquitoes and the air currents from an opening door. So can you.

PERCEPTION AND INTEGRATION WITH OTHER SENSES

Remember those eye rays and vibes I mentioned a few pages back? Although mainstream science does not yet recognize any form of individual nonassisted perception, other than by the accepted five senses, various scientific instruments clearly show that all humans and animals generate an electromagnetic field. Medical science detects and uses this field in various ways, such as electroencephalograms and electrocardiograms to detect disease and defibrillators to restart a heart in cardiac arrest. This electromagnetic field we generate is an energy field that Taoist adepts have been aware of and have used in practical ways for centuries.

Millions of individuals over all of recorded history have reported that they can perceive this field by "feeling" it—as in those eye rays. Millions of others report that they can feel the electromagnetic energy given off by power lines. Mainstream science has rejected these reports as anecdotal. This is understandable, due to the strictures and limitations of science and the lack of funding to develop research projects to study an individual's ability to detect electromagnetic fields. It was only recently that science became able to detect human electromagnetic fields; instruments such as defibrillators and ECG machines were developed only a few decades ago.

However, the fact that science lacks the means to measure certain phenomena does not mean that those phenomena do not exist. As examples, atomic radiation has existed since the beginning of time, somewhat earlier than the invention of the Geiger counter; the ancient Greeks, around 450 BC, developed atomic theory two and a half millennia before the invention of the laser that allows the visual observation of atoms. Science is simply a tool, and often late on the scene; a tool that provides many benefits but not all the answers, or perhaps even all the questions.

Taoist philosophy and science has recognized various forms of perception beyond the five senses since its inception in the fourth century BC, and centuries of Taoist experimentation developed methodology that has shown that certain forms of perception can be, like other senses, developed and improved by individual training. One of the most common forms of perception is the detection of a person's or an animal's energy when you cannot see, hear or smell them. For some individuals, that perceptive ability allows them to sense a person at considerable distance.

I do not claim that practicing the exercises that follow will enable you to announce that Aunt Matilda in Australia is coming to visit next month. What I have experienced and seen is that some students who have practiced these exercises diligently have developed extremely heightened perceptive abilities. I've also seen other students, apparently equally dedicated students, fail to develop their ability to perceive energy beyond the most basic level, and still others who were *never* able to develop this ability. Perhaps innate ability or talent is required to develop extended perception. Or perhaps it's a matter of dedicated practice. To excel at this art, perhaps both are required. Even the most talented athletes who do not practice likely do not go to the Olympics.

Motivation also plays a part. Sergeant Leon Jarozewski, a veteran of World War II, including parachute jumps into combat in Sicily and Normandy and various irregular actions, told me that to survive in combat you had to learn to *feel* the other guys before you could see them. He also said you should be lucky. One of my teachers in Hong Kong once told me to "cultivate luck." But that's a topic for another book. For now, we'll focus on learning to "feel the other guys before you can see them."

Most can develop this sense to the extent that it becomes useful. My intention is to pass on skills that can aid in survival, not to develop advanced adepts. I have limited the exercises in this chapter to those that are most commonly successful in reaching this goal.

The goal of the first exercise is to *see* the electromagnetic energy generated by a person. This ability is quite rare. A few, very few, seem to be able to do this naturally; a few others after a good bit of practice. Most of us are never able to *see* this energy. The advantages of being able to *see* energy, including being able to *see* a person's or an animal's energy in the dark, are obvious. But no matter if you cannot achieve this. *Seeing* energy can be a shortcut to feeling it, but it can also be a distraction. With practice most can at least learn to *feel* energy by practicing the following exercises, and that's more important. I only include this first exercise to *see* energy for the benefit of those rare individuals who can develop this ability. *Feeling* energy is something most of us can learn to do.

In future exercises and lessons, including field lessons, I will not refer to *seeing* energy visually. If you have or develop this ability you will naturally use it along with the ability to feel energy. For the rest of us, when I refer to *seeing* energy, I mean perceiving or feeling it.

These exercises are a step-by-step process. You may find that some are easier for you than others because perception is a sense not consciously used by many. Although most feel eye rays and vibes, few are really aware that this is an actual sense, and fewer still cultivate it. Just as you can train your eyes to see more detail, you can train your perception to be more sensitive. Different people also have varying levels of energy. I know more than one person whose personal energy stops battery-powered watches on their wrists. Also, as we will see in later exercises and lessons, people have different kinds of energy or vibes.

Exercise 1

*S*it *comfortably in a dimly lighted room. Have a friend sit somewhere easily seen. Make sure your friend is also comfortable and willing to sit still for at least seven minutes.*

Breathe, center and enter Tao space. Unfocus your eyes and look at the edge of your friend's body, letting your gaze drift over arms and shoulders. Keep your eyes soft. Use your peripheral vision to trace the outline of your friend's body. Slowly, slowly, breathing deeply and letting thoughts drift away, move your eyes so that you see your friend only from the corners of your eyes. Keep your attention focused and your eyes unfocused. Do not be in a hurry to see anything. Do not try to force anything. Relax, be in the moment and let your mind drift along with your vision. Continue for at least seven minutes, longer if your friend is cooperative. Did you see a faint glow come into view around your friend's body? If so, you're seeing the electromagnetic field that surrounds all of us.

Unless you have a natural talent for this, you may not see this field on the first try. A very small percentage of those who persist come to see this field, usually after a great deal of work. Others, most of us, simply cannot see this energy. You won't know if you can unless you try.

Exercise 2

The second exercise, and the most basic to learning to feel energy, is a variation of an exercise familiar to many practitioners of Tai Chi and Chi Gung. Although some forms of Tai Chi are taught as a martial art, both Tai Chi and Chi Gung are focused on aligning breath, movement and awareness to cultivate energy and good health. Sound familiar?

This exercise also requires the cooperation of a friend. Stand facing one another. Have your friend extend both hands towards you palms up. Sink into the standing position you are now familiar with. Breathe, center and enter Tao space. Extend your hands palms down over your friend's hands so that your palms are about three to four inches apart.

Visualize energy flowing from your friend's hands. The object is to feel your friend's energy. Move your hands slightly, back and forth and up and down, to better feel the energy radiating from your friend's hands. Direct your attention to focus on the very surface of your palms and fingers so that those nerve endings become highly sensitive. At first you may feel body heat rising from your friend's hands. If so, move your hands away until you cannot feel body heat. Energy gives off a more subtle feeling than heat. Although similar to heat, it is more of a feeling of slight vibration or pushing. Continue to direct all your attention to the surface of your palms and fingers. Do not try to force the feeling. Just keep your attention focused and directed and allow your hands to feel the energy. Continue for at least seven minutes.

When you tire, rest. Repeat as many times as the two of you are comfortable with. Some can feel energy at once; others require many sessions.

Exercise 3

Have your friend turn around so that you're both facing in the same direction. Your friend can either sit in a chair or stand. Relax into the standing position you are now familiar with. Breathe, center and enter Tao space.

Place your palms about three to four inches from your friend's shoulders. Direct your attention to your palms and fingers. Move your hands slowly back and forth across your friend's neck, shoulders and upper back. Focus all of your attention on your palms and fingers and feel them growing more and more sensitive. Breathe deeply. Do not force anything. Allow yourself to feel this energy. Continue this exercise for at least seven minutes, longer if you can. Repeat as many times as needed to feel the energy.

After some success with this exercise, take a step back and stand with your palms facing your friend's back. Continue to direct your attention to the surface of your palms and fingers, making them ever more sensitive. Continue until you can feel the energy while standing a step away. Then expand your field of sensitivity by moving your hands up and down to feel energy radiating from your friend's entire body.

Little by little, continue to increase the distance between you and your friend, but only to the limits of your ability to feel the energy. As you move away, the feeling of the energy will become fainter and more subtle, like music heard from far away. With time and consistent practice many can learn to feel a person's energy from across a room. To check yourself, as you move away, close your eyes and see if you can feel where your friend is.

Exercise 4

For this exercise we will expand sensitivity from your hands to your entire body. You may sit or stand, whichever is most comfortable for you. Close your eyes or use a handkerchief or scarf to block your vision. Ask your friend to quietly move to a random location in the room. Breathe, center and enter Tao space.

The next step is similar to the touch and skin sensitizing exercises you completed in the previous chapter. In fact, as you did those exercises you were developing perception, not only touch or skin sense. Having done those exercises you have taken steps towards making your entire being sensitive to energy radiation.

Direct your attention to the surface of your body. Start with your face, then direct your attention down over your neck, your shoulders, down your arms to your elbows, forearms, hands and fingertips, down your torso and over your thighs, knees, shins and calves to your feet and then toes. Visualize the skin over your entire body as having nerve endings extending slightly, microscopically, from each pore. Take enough time with this step to see and feel those nerve endings.

Next, from the skin with its nerve endings over your entire body, extend your awareness. Reach out for the subtle waves of energy you felt in previous exercises, scanning the room to detect your friend's energy. If you locate your friend by sound, either use earplugs or put your hands over your ears. If you feel your friend's energy, point in that direction to check the validity of your perception. If you're correct, you've taken a big step forwards. In either event, ask your friend to move to another location as quietly as possible and repeat the exercise.

Do the exercise for at least seven minutes, longer if you wish. Repeat as needed.

Exercise 5

This "stealth" exercise is one that most often turns into a game that everyone enjoys, one that most of us played variations of when we were children. But make no mistake: although this can be an enjoyable game, it's also deadly serious. Being able to detect a person of ill intent before you can see them could save your life one day.

Sit or stand in the center of a room, the larger the better, or outside in your yard or other private place. Cover your eyes and ears. Breathe, center and enter Tao space. Follow the directions in Exercise 4 to activate your sensitivity.

Ask your friend to move quietly and slowly and attempt to get close to you and touch you undetected. Reach out as previously to feel your friend's energy. As soon as you feel it, point to the location you perceive it to be coming from. Whether you are successful or not, repeat the exercise.

A variation is to invite a group to do this exercise, or play this game, however you prefer to think of it. Have one person sit or stand in the center of a large circle made up of the others. One person at a time, in random order, attempts to sneak up and touch the person in the center before being detected. Take turns being in the center.

It might surprise you how effective this simple exercise can be—if you've done the foundation work leading up to this point. I've seen many different groups engage in this exercise, from combat veterans and martial artists to suburban housewives in self-defense classes. Almost everyone—if they've done the previous exercises—is able to increase their sensitivity to the presence of others.

Exercise 6

Remember the game Where's Waldo? We've often called this the "Waldo Game" to loosen up tense students. As I've previously written, being relaxed is key to success in these exercises. Being tense and anxious is a barrier to success.

This exercise is designed to expand your perception of energy beyond your immediate space. You will again need the help of a friend to get started. Sit comfortably in one room and ask your friend go to another room, but to not tell you which room. Breathe, center and enter Tao space. Follow the directions in Exercise 4 to activate your sensitivity. Extend your awareness to feel all the rooms in your house. Adjust the instructions accordingly if you're in an apartment, or if you do this exercise outside. The goal is to extend your awareness as far as you can so that you can feel anyone enter your space.

Do not visualize the various rooms or try to guess where your friend might be. Simply relax, breathe, stay in Tao space and extend your sensitivity and awareness from your body to encompass the entire house. Some find it helpful to visualize a bubble surrounding you and then expanding that bubble to include the entire house or apartment. Most find success at this skill by simply extending their attention.

As soon as you feel your friend's energy, go to that location. If you do not feel the energy, continue the exercise for at least seven minutes. Rest and repeat.

If you encounter a lack of initial success, try sitting comfortably in a dark room and focus your eyes and your attention on a candle flame. Let your mind wander, drift like a feather on the wind. Let it wander outside the room and through the rooms in your house, or out through a window or door or even the roof. Let your mind drift all around you. Search gently and softly for energy within your area of awareness.

Some find that they can develop this skill quickly. For a few it comes naturally and easily. For others, acquiring this skill requires concentrated, persistent effort over an extended period. If you do not get it quickly, continue to repeat the exercise and devote consistent but relaxed time to achieving success. Do not overconcentrate. This is not a matter of willpower and forcing yourself to feel. It's more a case of allowing yourself to feel.

Perception is one of the most important survival skills. Developing this level of sensitivity to energy not only informs you when someone is in your space, it could aid you if you ever have to locate a lost child, or a person in a building filled with smoke. As in the stealth exercise, make this a game. In your spare time, center and enter Tao space and extend your awareness all around you.

Future lessons will not repeat breathing, centering and entering Tao space instructions. You have mastered these basics, so simply center and enter within one breath and proceed with the new exercise. Nor will we repeat the instructions for developing each of your senses. You have also mastered those skills and it's now time to move on.

INTERACTING WITH YOUR ENVIRONMENT

TAKING YOUR SKILLS OUTSIDE

Exercise

The preceding lessons were designed to be done in or around your home. Now let's go to the world outside. Pick a spot where you can sit comfortably and securely: a park, a country field, or a sidewalk café—anyplace where you can sit for a period of time without being disturbed. Bring with you a notebook and pen or pencil.

After selecting your spot, relax, enter Tao space and extend *all* your senses: sight, sound, smell, skin sense and perception. Start with your immediate area, then extend as far as you can comfortably. Remaining relaxed and in Tao space, *see* everything in your space—everything. Note everything you see with your eyes, hear, smell, feel, perceive. Each blade of grass, each flower, each rock, each person and car or truck is different and worthy of observation. Allow all your senses to open and be receptive. *See* as much as you can, scanning with your eyes and perception. Sit still and quietly, scanning, seeing, smelling, listening and absorbing for at least seven minutes. Longer is better, if you're relaxed and not forcing anything. This should be enjoyable.

At the end of seven minutes or an extended period, take out your notebook and write down what you have seen and sensed. Try to remember everything, visualizing as needed. Try to recall all details of everything. What color was that young woman's dress? How tall was she? What color were her eyes? How many pigeons were fluttering about, and were all of them healthy or did one of them have an injured leg? Did the road smell hot, as tarmac does in the sun, or did you smell new mown grass, or roses, or jasmine? Was the grass well watered, green and lush, or dried out, sparse and brown? Where was that trail of ants going and what were they carrying? If there was a rose, how many petals did it have and *what color was it: red, pink, white? Did you hear a horn honk, a sparrow chirp, children laughing? Did you perceive those people walking on the sidewalk behind you, the kid on the skateboard before he rounded the corner into your view? Was there a rooster in the seat next to you, a Roman candle under your chair?*

You will find that you'll only be able to write down broad strokes. Detailing all that there is to see in your yard, or from your balcony or patio, or in any place at all, a sidewalk café or a bus stop, would require an encyclopedia. Writing down all you could see of one blade of grass could require many lines. Describing one ant and its activities at least a page or two. Your goal here is not to write a book about your immediate environment. Writing down what you see helps to focus, to understand and remember how complex the world around us is. There are a thousand dramas taking place this moment within a few yards of where you sit.

It's impossible to take in all that life brings to us, unless we're in a transcendent state of being. Our senses function as filters. Without the filters of our senses we would be overwhelmed. What we have been working on in the previous lessons is refining your senses and clearing your filters, the goal being to increase your awareness of the world around you and everything in it, and to come to understand and appreciate our world in all its splendor. And yes, that's a major survival skill—perhaps the most important one.

BIRDS AND BEES, DOGS, CATS AND LIZARDS

Observing animals and their behavior enables us to better understand them and react accordingly. Animal observation will also aid you if you hunt or fish, whether by choice or necessity. Animal observations, aside from being of direct value, also help to develop observational skills that will aid in understanding more complex creatures—humans.

Some people are frightened of all dogs, some of snakes, others of bees or spiders. Fear clouds perceptions and can lead to inappropriate responses, such as running away or attacking when there's no reason to do either. We'll deal with fear in a separate exercise further along in the book, but for now set aside fears you might have of animals, unless those fears get in the way of the following exercises. If your fears of animals run deep and you cannot set them aside, first work through the exercises in the section titled "Fear" (page 106) to work on overcoming your fears, then come back to these exercises.

PETS

If you have a pet, begin by closely observing your pet's activities for an extended period, at least thirty minutes. Few people have ever directed their attention so closely to the animals that share their living space. Doing so might be a revelation.

Exercise

Sit or stand comfortably, enter Tao space and direct your senses—sight, sound, smell, skin sense and perception—to your pet. Select a time of day when your pet is active; watching it sleep for a half hour won't be very useful. Be prepared to remain centered and move if needed to follow it. Watch all its actions, how it moves its legs, where it walks and why. Did it move to avoid bright sunlight or a cold draft, or to go to its food? What attracted its attention—a knock at the door, the radio, a bird at the window? Did something surprise it? Study its facial expressions and body language and feel its energy. Is it confident or tentative, friendly or shy, aggressive or passive?

After observing your pet, in your notebook describe it in detail and record its activities, mannerisms and personality. Did its behavior surprise you in any way, and if so, how?

FERAL ANIMALS

Exercise

If you have no pets, or have already completed the previous exercise, now go outside and observe creatures in their own habitat. No matter where you live you can find undomesticated animals. In the stone canyons of Manhattan you can watch pigeons living their lives, and hawks taking them in flight. Where do those pigeons feed and nest? How do they avoid hawks? How do hawks hunt pigeons? What is the difference between a pigeon's energy and a hawk's? Watch a lizard sunning itself on a rock and see its eyes, absent of feeling and constantly scanning. Why does the lizard sun itself? Why does it constantly scan its sur-roundings?

Some people confuse bees with wasps, but they are entirely different crea-tures, and often mortal enemies. Bees live on nectar; they have enormous eyes and look back at you when you look at them. Bees have their own affairs to tend to and are not very interested in you. Watch a bee, or a few bees, even for seven minutes and you'll learn a great deal, not only about bees, but also the immediate environment. Wasps are ill-tempered, meat-eating predators. Watch them with care. Generally speaking they will not bother you unless you bother them—you are not their prey. However, it can be difficult to determine what might bother them. Just be sure to stay out of their way, but do watch them—see them—and feel the different kinds of energy they generate. You'll learn more than you might imagine, and not only about wasps.

In your notebook describe the creatures you have observed and their activity. What have you learned about them?

WILDLIFE

To observe wildlife in its habitat requires, first, that you find them; that you possess acute observational skills, which you have developed in the previous lessons; and that you have the ability to be unobserved by the wildlife. In a later section, "Being Unseen or Seen" (page 99), we'll learn the art of "being not seen." Some learn this so well they can become virtually invisible, or at least forgettable. But for now we'll expand a little on what we have already learned in developing our senses, as well as learning to be still in Tao space. This lesson is a big step forward in that it not only requires these skills, but is a real-world exercise that will test your grasp of fundamentals and allow you to use them in a natural environment.

Exercise

To expand your observation abilities and develop your ability to locate wild animals, which in a survival situation could be critical, go to a mountain, woodland, desert or beach—whatever wild area you can find near you. If there is no wild area near you, marginal areas will do. Even a fringe of trees or bushes beside a freeway has wild creatures living in it, as do vacant lots, overgrown hillsides and beaches a little way from the crowds.

Some suburban neighborhoods have many wild creatures living in them: possums, raccoons, coyotes, deer, and in some areas even bears and mountain lions. Few suburban dwellers have any idea that they are sharing their neighborhood with wild creatures. For the purposes of this exercise it's best to go to an unfamiliar area rather than staying in your own neighborhood, even if it's overrun with wildlife. You can observe those creatures whenever you wish, and they are accustomed to your presence.

Think of this exercise as hunting without taking the animal. Obviously if you do hunt, for survival or otherwise, this skill will be critical. It helps if you have some idea of the kind of animal that might be living in your chosen area, or, you might say, "hunting ground."

When you reach your chosen hunting ground, let the patterns of thought you have used to get there slip away as you walk away from your vehicle. Forget about the highway, the traffic, and the idiot who cut you off at the intersection. Forget about work. Let the familiar constrictions of mind slip away as you move into the natural world and prepare to enter it and become part of it.

Find a place that feels right to you and stop. Note where the wind is coming from. You should select your spot so you can direct your attention upwind, in the direction the wind is coming from. The wind will carry your scent downwind, and every creature downwind with a nose will sense your presence and avoid you.

If you're unfamiliar with the natural world, you might be a little nervous or anxious. You might have concerns about bears or mountain lions. It's unlikely you'll be attacked, but use common sense. If, for example, signs are posted warning of mountain lions, as there are in many Southern California parks, find another place for this exercise.

Choose a spot where you can see without being seen, and where your outline is obscured by something behind you: a large rock, a tree or bushes. Sit in a comfortable position, as you do when entering Tao space in your home or outside on a park bench or in a café. Find that place within you where stillness lives: Tao space. After entering Tao space, allow yourself to blend with and become part of whatever is nearest to you. If, for example, you're sitting with your back to an oak tree, relax into the tree and become part of it. Visualize your body as being inside the tree trunk. If you're leaning against a desert boulder overlooking a water hole, see your body sinking back into the rock. Become part of the world around you.

Once you are comfortably blended with the selected natural feature, direct your attention to the immediate environment. Extend all your senses and see what there is to see, pinecones or rabbit droppings, a blue jay's feather, tracks of . . . what, a dog or a coyote? Don't overanalyze these details. Note them and continue to scan.

Keeping your eyes open, extend your awareness as far as you can, across meadows, through woods, up the mountainside. Wherever you happen to be, extend your awareness to its fullest. Feel the wind moving, smell the cold granite or musty leaves or the tannin from the dark swampy stream behind you. Hear the skittering of dry leaves, the breathing of the fox that's watching you, the drip of early morning dew from the limbs above you. Embody stillness.

Now visualize the animals that you think might be in the area: deer, rabbit, squirrel, crow or field mouse. See the creatures as if they were standing in front of you. Retain full awareness of your surroundings but focus on visualizing particular animals. Success will come more quickly if you have an idea of what kind of animal is likely to be in your area and you visualize only that one animal.

Once you have fully visualized an animal, or a number of different animals, mentally ask it or them to come to you. Visualize the animal feeling your request and being drawn to you. This action generates energy, a kind of energy that can draw animals to you. Having a particular kind of animal in mind will generate specific energy on a particular wavelength. Tension, fear or predatory thoughts will neutralize this energy. Remain in Tao space and simply ask the wildlife to come to you.

Continue to watch and see and feel everything around you, above you and under you. Do not move. You might think you're not moving, but you probably are moving. A deer can spot the flicker of an eyelid at fifty yards. Cultivate stillness in your entire body and let your mind be as still as a forest pond. Sink deep into your place and be part of it. Let flies or mosquitoes be, do not swat them. If you get cold or hot let those sensations pass through you. You'll learn more about how to allow cold or heat to pass through you in later lessons. For now, simply remain in Tao space and let those body feelings go.

If your visualization is clear, your energy request strong and there are in fact animals in the area, you might find the animal you visualized in front of you. This does not work every time. But it does work often enough to insure hunting success for hunters in many so-called primitive societies.

This is not magic. This is a method taught by shamans to hunters in early societies around the world since prehistory, and codified by Taoist shamans in ancient times. I have hunted with native hunters in Asia who used these exact methods, along with all the hunter's skills and tools, to feed their families consistently and successfully.

When I hunted elk for the first time, after many years of Taoist training, I sat with my back against an aspen and entered Tao space. It was November at a high altitude in the Rocky Mountains with patches of snow everywhere. I had folded a blanket to sit on, but in time the cold came up through it. At first I was cold. After a while the cold passed through me and I wasn't cold. My nose itched. Then it didn't. I sank back into the tree and became the tree. My roots grew deep into the ground and I stretched my limbs wide and watched the days and nights pass.

Of course, in consensual reality I didn't really sit there for days and become part of the tree. I visualized blending with the tree and let time be time without measure. In doing so I subsumed my consciousness into the tree and ceased radiating a hunter's energy. In effect I created a cloak of invisibility. We sat together, the tree and I, until only the tree remained. After some time, a bull elk and his herd of does walked by me, passing no more than ten feet from where I sat. They never saw me.

Obviously, the ability to blend into your surroundings can be valuable in ways other than watching wildlife—such as hiding from pursuers. A related topic is controlling your own energy field, which we'll learn to do later in this book.

ASSESSING PEOPLE AND THEIR INTENTIONS

Knowing others is wisdom;
Knowing the self is enlightenment.
—Lao Tze

Does anyone ever truly know another person, ever see into their deepest heart? I'll leave that question to philosophers, who have pondered it over the ages. What we are concerned with in this book is improving our ability to read other people, their characters and intentions, whether good or ill. Like the other skills in this book, further developing your natural ability to assess another person's intentions serves two purposes: it could save your life, or that of a loved one; and it can certainly enhance your relationships.

Much of who we are, who we've been and what we are about to do is written in our faces, displayed in our posture and movements, and radiated in the energy we give off. Most of us wear masks that we show to the world, masks developed over our lifetimes, masks that we hide behind. Through life experience some of us can, to a certain extent, see the person behind the mask. But perceptive people can see through those masks and read others like the proverbial open book; see their pasts, their characters and predict their behavior.

As some are gifted with athletic abilities, certain people have a gift for perception. Others simply pay close attention to other people. Some do both. However, many people are so self-involved that they do not give others much, if any, attention. Others are so concerned with the impression they are making they only see others as an audience for the drama of their own lives. Some simply are blind to others and cannot see them beyond obvious physical features, as a visually blind person cannot see color. There are those who do not even notice things that are as plain as the nose on your face. Recently my wife and I had lunch with two women friends we know well. In company with family, we've traveled together and spent much time in each other's company. One of them lived in the same house with my family and me for about a month. The day before we met them for lunch I had my hair cut short and my beard trimmed closely, as I do in summer. I've worn a beard for years and neither woman had ever seen me without it. When we all sat down together, one woman said, "Oh, wow, you've cut your hair really short and your beard is trimmed so close. Did you do that because it's so hot?" The other woman was telling a long story and simply said, "Hello." Ten minutes later, after her story ended, she looked at me and said, "Did you grow a beard?" This woman had not noticed the most superficial and highly visible thing about my appearance. Did she have any idea of my character? How could she be sure I wasn't an ax murderer?

Some years ago I was having a late-night conversation with a group of friends. We were all standing on a balcony overlooking a deep canyon and the lights of a large city. One of my friends, Fred, had had way too much to drink and had become argumentative. We had all seen Fred behave like this previously. But never, although he had some history as a violent person, had he crossed the line from verbal argument and belligerence to violence. Fred, a large, strong man and experienced fighter, was focused on Sam, an average-sized fellow who enjoyed discussing politics from an academic, detached point of view. Sam was leaning against a rather low railing. Fred's end of the discussion grew louder. I noticed him slide his left foot forward an inch or so and slightly curl the fingers of his right hand. I stepped up to Fred, put my arm around his shoulder and pulled him tightly to me, taking his balance. I smiled, said I was hungry and asked him to come inside with me and help me find some barbequed ribs. The interruption was enough to distract him. He led me into the house, ate a bite or two and fell asleep on a couch. No one else noticed Fred's intention or the significance of my intervention. The next morning Fred came to me, shaking, hung over and remorseful, and thanked me for stepping in: "Man, if I'd hit Sam he would have gone right over the balcony."

In previous lessons you have learned to perceive energy and to closely observe inanimate objects, animals and people. In these lessons we will focus on perceiving different kinds of energy, as well as closely observing the physical being of people.

There are various systems that attempt to detect a person's nature and their intentions, and whether they're lying or telling the truth, by analyzing certain facial and body movements. These systems *might be* useful for trained professionals in a controlled environment such as an interrogation room, and with members of their own culture. Such systems are highly dependent on cultural norms and break down in assessing persons from other cultures, or even subcultures. In addition, in their attempts to develop a standardized model of behavior, these systems fail to allow for individual variations in manner, thereby introducing large amounts of error into their calculations and rendering their systems about as reliable as phrenology. Further, those systems completely ignore the perception of individual energy, something most of us do to some degree intuitively, because they cannot fit it into their standardized model.

The Tao method is to use directed attention, energy sensing and intuition, building on skills that virtually all of us have developed since infancy. One of my teachers once told me, "The eyes don't lie." He did not mean the eyes of another. He meant that my own eyes could always see the truth of a person, if I allowed them to. Over the years I have found that to be true, except when I deceived myself about a person's nature, as most of us do sometimes.

In these lessons you will perceive what kind of energy a person radiates—light or dark, hard or soft, cool or hot, comforting or edgy, angry or calm. Feeling the nature of individual energy is a step beyond simply feeling energy—an important one, and one you've likely already experienced. Unless you have no perceptive ability at all, there have been times when you felt either comfortable or uncomfortable around a person you just met; times when someone just felt wrong; times when you reacted with suspicion; times when you felt immediate trust. We will build on those feelings and your natural intuition by first perceiving energy, then staying with it and feeling it more deeply.

Add your visual observational abilities and your other sense abilities such as hearing to your ability to perceive energy and you have a powerful array of tools to enable you to determine a person's nature and immediate intentions.

SELF-ASSESSMENT

Before we direct our attention to assessing other people, we should first do a self-assessment. If we don't know ourselves, how can we know others? Most of us think we know ourselves quite well. But for almost all of us there are aspects of our inner selves that we are not consciously aware of. It's useful in everyday life to know these things about ourselves. And if you've not been in a survival situation you might wonder how you'd react, how well you'd hold up under life-threatening stress. Only actual experience will fully answer that question, but a close, unsparing and rigorous self-appraisal will help to answer it. There are also aspects of our inner selves we think are concealed from others, things about our character and background that only we know. Perhaps that's a good thing, perhaps not. Let's first take a close look at our physical selves and our energy.

Exercise

Go to a full-length mirror. You do not need to set an alarm for a fixed period. Continue this exercise for as long as you need to see and perceive the person in the mirror. Stand closely before the mirror, so close you can see only your face. Later you'll step back so you can see your whole body, but we start with the face.

Breathe, center and slip into Tao space. Direct all of your attention to the reflection in the mirror. Think of your face as the face to objectify it. Scan the entire face, hairline to chin, ear to ear. Note carefully the lifelines on the forehead, at the brow, the corners of the eyes, the mouth. Note how the mouth is held. Are the eyebrows raised or lowered? What do those lines and features tell you? Is this a face that smiles a great deal, or one that frowns? Are there any scars? Is this the face of a person who carries anger, or resentment? Look deep into the eyes. Are they opaque and closed to the world or open?

As when you first looked at, and then came to see, flowers, rocks and other objects of attention, allow yourself to sink into the face to see all details and to absorb the essence of this face. Open your perception and feel the energy given off by this face.

Now move back a step or two so you can see the body from toes to top of the head. Does this person stand straight or lean forward, or to the rear or one side? Are there injuries or impairments that prevent straight posture? Is the head held high or carried forward or bent low? Is one shoulder higher than the other? Are the hands open or closed?

What do you see and feel about this face and body, this person? Is this person confident or tentative, friendly or shy, aggressive or passive? What is written on this face: anxiety or ease, anger or contentment, kindness or selfishness? Do you see compassion and openness, or fear and armor; determination or indifference; perseverance or vacillation; strength or weakness; arrogance or humility? See deeply behind the face and body of the adult and see the child that still lives *inside. Was the child wounded? How deeply? Did the child have a mostly happy life, or one marked by sadness, cruelty or indifference?*

For some, this exercise can be a profound experience, leading to new insights about the self, perhaps to emotional pain and tears. Whatever your personal experience, stay with this exercise until you *see* this person and the spirit inside of it. Whatever you see will be of value to you. If you see a face and body that seems to show confidence and strength, ask yourself if it's overconfidence and surface strength that you see. If you see a face and body that seems to show weakness and fear, and you wonder if this person is a survivor, take heart. We all have fears, and in a later exercise we'll learn how to overcome them and become stronger by doing so.

Have you ever heard your recorded voice and think, "That doesn't sound like my voice?" If the recording was of reasonable fidelity, it *did* sound like your voice. It's a good exercise to listen closely to a recording of your voice with the same level of directed attention you brought to the mirror exercise. Listen to timber, tone, volume and enunciation. What does your voice say about who you are?

As an additional exercise, have a friend or family member video you as you go about your day. Direct your attention to something other than the camera. The idea is to capture some footage of yourself when you are not playing to the camera. Then view the footage. Watch how you walk, enter rooms, reach for things. Then ask yourself the same questions as in the mirror exercise. Odds are you'll learn a great deal about yourself. Such self-knowledge leads to a better understanding of what qualities you need to develop to be a better survivor.

ASSESSING OTHER PEOPLE

Some psychopaths—violent and nonviolent, serial killers and con men—are adept at concealing what they are, their lack of human feeling and their intentions. But those individuals are few and far between. Most psychopaths radiate energy that makes even those who are not especially perceptive edgy. Except for extremely well-guarded psychopaths, you can assess most people by using the methods with which you are now familiar: centered and fully directed attention, focused senses including perception, and intuition. And even psychopaths can be perceived with well-developed and concentrated focus. Keep in mind that people are highly complex, have many sides and cannot be easily summed up. But for our immediate purposes we can learn to see what we need to see of people and their intentions.

Exercise 1

Ask a family member or close friend to be your person of attention, to sit quietly where you can observe them as you have various objects of attention. Since we are drawing on the patience of another person, set your alarm for seven minutes, a long time for an untrained person to sit still. You will find that it's difficult to objectively assess a person with whom you're very familiar. As in the mirror exercise, try to objectify them and see them for the first time.

Sit comfortably, breathe, center, enter Tao space and direct all your attention to this person. As when assessing yourself, minutely observe the details and features of their face and its overall essence. See how the features are formed: lips, nose, eyes and eyebrows. Look carefully at their lifelines. Focus deeply on their eyes. Draw on what you learned while doing your personal assessment. Open your perception and feel their energy. Let your gaze drift over their entire body. What is the nature of their posture? Do they sit straight or sprawled, legs crossed, tucked under them?

Ask yourself what experiences and what kind of inner life have shaped this person's features and drawn their lifelines. What is their expression at rest? Do you see and feel good humor, anger, fear, confidence, placidity, animation, spite, goodwill? What does this person's face and resting body reveal about their character?

After seven minutes, call time on the exercise, thank the person who helped and then continue to observe them as they stand and go about their business. Do they stand straight or bent? Do they lean to one side? If they stand crooked, is their posture due to bodily pain or something else? Observe their walk. Do they stride forward with confidence or do they step tentatively and unsurely? Do they move athletically or are they awkward and uncoordinated in movement? What is the nature of their voice? Is it loud or quiet, soft or grating to the ear? What does its tone and timbre tell you? Do they lecture or speak forcefully? Do they smell of perfume, sweat, food, wet dogs? Most importantly, what kind of energy do you feel radiating from them?

Exercise 2

Next, pick another family member or friend, ask them to be your person of attention, and, after slipping into Tao space, focus your directed attention and perception on them for one minute. Focus tightly and with full concentration. After doing this once, shorten the time to a few seconds and repeat. The visual and other skills you have previously learned will come into play. After a few exercises you'll be able to get a quick reading on a person in seconds. Obviously you'll be able to learn more if you have more time. But it's vital to be able to get a quick reading on a person.

Exercise 3

Continuing in a comfortable environment and with family members or friends, the third stage is to do quick readings of persons of attention without staring at them. Glance at them and look away quickly. Look at them from out of the corners of your eyes. Talk to them and carry on a conversation while seeing them and perceiving their energy without being obvious. Do as many of these exercises as you need or want to, keeping in mind that you are working with familiar people and that you are most likely getting benign readings.

Next you'll be directing your attention to strangers without their knowledge. You can learn a great deal about a person by simply being in their presence for a short time and, if attuned to it, feeling their energy. Even at some distance and without perceiving energy you can determine quite a lot about a person by simple but careful observation.

Once at a trade show a few exhibitors gathered in my booth to pass the time. With nothing else to do I devised a little game. An entrance to the nearby restrooms was covered by a heavy curtain. Many people passed in and out. We would observe people as they passed through the curtain and see if we could determine which person was a company owner and which were employees. This was a trade show where there were many small companies and therefore many company owners. One of our number agreed to station himself next to the curtain and confirm with the people coming out whether they owned a company or not. Some people strode through the curtain, brushing it aside with an arm. Others stopped at the curtain, hesitated, pulled the curtain aside, then after determining that the way was clear, went in. Every person who brushed the curtain aside and walked through without hesitating was a company owner. The others were employees. No exceptions.

Here is a much more serious example. A young woman who was a fellow martial arts student was standing at a bus stop after a night class when a van pulled up. The side door opened and a man stepped out. In a flash, although she had never seen him or the driver before and they at first displayed no overt signs of aggression or ill intent, she was able to immediately *see* them and sense their intentions. She readied herself, and as the man reached for her she took immediate and forceful defensive action. By doing so she saved herself from violation, injury and possibly death. She reported the incident to the police. When the man she had encountered showed up at the emergency room for treatment he was arrested. Interrogation, and confessions, revealed that the two men had raped a series of young women in the area.

ON THE STREET

Once you are at ease with assessing friends and family at home or in other comfortable places it's time to go to the world outside, as you previously did when observing objects and undomesticated animals. You'll find that in many ways it's easier to assess strangers than family and friends, partially because you're starting with a clean slate; you don't have knowledge of the person and don't have to see a familiar person as if for the first time.

Exercise 1

Pick a spot where you can sit comfortably and where there are many people passing, perhaps an outdoor café or a mall food court. Settle in and do what everyone else is doing: people watching—but with a difference.

If you've done all the previous lessons you have a firm foundation in seeing and perceiving. Think of this as a graduation exercise or a final exam. While directing your attention to persons out in the world, do not project your energy by staring fixedly at them. Doing so was fine at home with friends and family as basic lessons, but not out in the world. Remember those eye rays? You do not want to be mistaken for a stalker. Be casual. Be cool. Glance at your person of attention and look away. Look at them from out of the corners of your eyes and feel them. When you look at them straight on, do so for only a few moments. Let your eyes wander over the entire scene including your person of attention. Do not tunnel in on them and forget your surroundings.

After selecting your spot, relax, enter Tao space and extend all of your senses: sight, sound, smell, skin sense and perception. Start with your immediate area, then extend as far as you can comfortably. Remaining relaxed and in Tao space, scan everything and everyone in your immediate environment. Sit quietly and ease into the local environment—scanning, seeing, smelling, listening, absorbing.

After scanning all the people in your area, direct your attention to one person, maybe a man sitting alone. Look at him for a second or two and then look away, but continue to focus your attention on him for a few moments—then cut away and scan, while thinking about what you perceived of that person. Let your gaze drift back to him, then away.

Mentally describe his physical features and facial features: height, weight, build, hair color; large mouth or small; long nose or short; large, round eyes or small, narrow ones. Is he muscular, wiry, soft bodied? How is he dressed: suit and tie or jeans; worn sneakers or shiny new shoes? From his clothing can you tell if he's local or a traveler? What do his lifelines and expression tell you about him? Does he habitually frown or smile? Are those worry lines around his eyes? Does he squint, perhaps from long hours in the sun? Is he deeply tanned, and if so is it a beach tan or the coloring of a person who works outside? See the child inside the adult. Was he a happy child, abused, a bully or bullied, popular, a loner, studious, fearful, confident?

Observe his behavior. Does he look around frequently, as if he's waiting for someone or watching to see if anyone is looking at him? Is he absorbed in eating and unaware of his surroundings, or does he scan the area or look out of the corners of his eyes as he eats? Is it a hot day, and if so, why is he wearing a jacket? How does he hold his hands? Are his hands dirty or scarred? Are they the hands of a construction worker or office worker? Is he a fighter? Is he poised, as if ready to get up, or slumped in his chair?

While observing all of these things, feel his energy. What kind of feelings does he project? Is he calm, relaxed, serene, agitated, nervous, edgy, angry, irritated? What general sense of him do you perceive? Does he carry a dark cloud; does he feel light, free, open? Do you sense any meanness in him? Does he feel trustworthy or shaky? Remember how that wasp's energy felt? Is this a predator? Would you be comfortable with him if he asked you to join him at his table for coffee?

This assessment should require no more than a minute. All of your previous lessons have started with lengthy periods, then gone to very short periods, seconds or split seconds. With only a little practice you should be able to do a flash assessment, enough to get a general impression, in a few seconds.

Exercise 2

After assessing your person of attention, scan the crowd and select another person of attention, perhaps a young mother with two children. Does she look *tired? Do her feet hurt? Does she smile when she looks at her children? Do her handbag, shoes and clothing look expensive? What kind of energy is she radiating? Aren't those kids cute and don't they put a smile on your face?*

Do a flash assessment and move on. Scan and focus, scan and focus, picking out individuals and assessing them. Working in this way will teach you to better see people as they are, and to do so quickly, and in crowds. You will also notice those who stand out from the crowd by dress, manner, behavior and energy. The middle-aged, overweight man in too-tight jeans striding through the café and giving off a nervous vibe, as if he's on a mission, maybe looking for a lost child, or his pet rooster. Those three teenage boys with pants down around their butts, talking loudly—what's their vibe? Are they looking for trouble or just being kids? That young man with the two-day stubble beard talking to the waitress—is he asking for a date or ordering coffee? The couple sitting close together and sharing a piece of chocolate cake and looking into each other's eyes—obviously young lovers. What about that woman who's been watching you while you've been assessing various people in the crowd? Is she a plainclothes security guard who picked up on your vibe, or did you meet her at the soccer game?

Exercise 3

Next, do these assessments while walking through various areas: malls, parking lots, sidewalks and parks. Scan and focus, scan and focus. Do not tunnel. People watching is a universal pastime, one carried on in every culture of the world. People are endlessly fascinating, and opening all of your senses to them makes them ever more so. After you become comfortable with seeing people in this way, you'll most likely find that it easily becomes a habit, and will serve you well when you meet a new person, conduct a job interview, or negotiate the terms of a deal or the price of anything.

There are systems that teach how to spot people who might be terrorists, criminals or otherwise dangerous. These systems might work for professionals. But they carry a heavy price. If the only tool you have is a hammer, everything looks like a nail. Professionals who spend their days looking for people of ill intent tend to become suspicious of everyone and sometimes come to believe that everyone is a criminal. True, many of the people they encounter in their work are criminals. But the practice of assessing everyone with only a yes-or-no, criminal-or-not method becomes corrosive in and of itself, and is ultimately damaging to the person who practices it. Statistics show that on average less than 0.7 percent of any population commits all violent crime. Most people are decent and well intentioned. By following the Tao you will come to better know the good people you meet, and be better able to spot those who might cause problems.

SURVIVAL-LEVEL PHYSICAL FITNESS

Have you ever seen a cat doing push-ups? Neither have I. If you've watched cats, you've probably noticed that all cats stretch with intensity. That's a hint about physical fitness. Street cats are in terrific physical condition and able to perform feats we humans cannot, no matter how hard we might try. Even house cats that lie around the house and move no further than their food bowl can perform physical feats beyond our abilities. But a house cat is no match for a street cat. That's also a hint. Ever wrestle a chimp? Do so and you'll learn how strong our simian cousins are. Chimps don't do push-ups either, or work out in a gym. What they do is swing from limbs, climb, run and jump. That's another hint.

Our muscle structure and physical makeup is different than that of a cat or a chimp, and we probably will have to do some push-ups and other physical exercise to be in survivor-level physical condition. But doing what cats, chimps and other animals do—concentrated muscle extension and contraction (stretching), walking, running, jumping and climbing—is a good place to start. Being completely sedentary, sitting in front of a computer or a television all day, is good training to become a couch potato; it is not a prescription for survival fitness.

Simply being conscious of your body and how it moves, directing your attention to it moving around your tan tien and using all of your muscles to their fullest as you go through your day—in other words fully occupying your body—will help to attain and maintain physical fitness. When you have watched people and how they moved, most likely you have observed those who moved as if their bodies were controlled by strings in the hands of an inept puppet master. Few of those people have physical handicaps; most are simply unaware of their own bodies and use them as they do a car—something to get them from place to place. Not all of us are gifted with perfect coordination, but all of us can benefit from directing our attention to our bodies and how we move. Watching athletes, or cats, who move smoothly, powerfully and gracefully and then emulating that kind of movement, adapted to our own bodies, will aid in getting fit and staying fit.

There are Chinese Kung Fu styles based on what is often termed the "five animals." There is little agreement among practitioners regarding how these styles came into being, or even what their true purpose is. Training to fight as a particular animal fights would seem to be counter-intuitive and not particularly useful. When I lived in Hong Kong, a professor of Chinese history, a highly trained adept in Chinese martial arts and healing, told me that one thing he was sure of about these systems and their history is that the conditioning exercises, which were based on observing animals, are efficient and effective. Having seen those who followed his training methods, I had to agree.

In this book we're not going into detail on esoteric conditioning. We'll focus on basics that can be done anywhere by anyone with no specialized equipment, can easily fit into your daily life, and which if done correctly will make you survival-fit. You do not need to be muscled like a bodybuilder, spend hours weekly at a gym or be conditioned to the top level of a specialized sport to be fit. Being survival-fit means that you are reasonably strong, fast, agile and flexible—within the limits of your body type and natural ability. Those limits might be much greater than you think.

Visualization, directed attention and intensity are the keys to achieving maximum results within the minimum amount of time. Done correctly, physical exercises are not only physical exercises; they are mind/body exercises. In the following exercises always move around your tan tien, direct your attention to your body and visualize the workings of your body. This process transforms ordinary exercises, such as muscle extensions and contractions, push-ups, sit-ups and so on, and produces extraordinary results.

While doing the exercises, remember to maintain correct body alignment by keeping your spine erect, visualizing a strong, flexible cable attached to the top of your head and holding the weight of your body, by flexing your lower abdominal muscles and tucking or rolling your tailbone under and to the front, and using your lower abdominal muscles to pull your pubic bone forward and slightly up, thereby tilting your pelvis and bringing it into proper alignment.

Before starting any physical training program, such as body weight exercises, you should do a personal assessment and determine at what level you should start. It doesn't matter if you can do one hundred push-ups or one. When doing the concentrated muscle extension and contraction exercises, for instance, you simply start at whatever level of conditioning you are at. What does matter is that you focus on your body and keep your attention directed to it and its abilities. If you are serious about training you'll need to push yourself beyond your abilities, but not to the point of injury. Save that final level of exertion for an actual survival situation.

CONCENTRATED MUSCLE EXTENSION AND CONTRACTION

If you've closely watched a cat stretch, you will have noticed that they extend and contract every muscle, even including each toe, with full intensity. We'll start with emulating those kinds of extensions and contractions, of course adapted to our own bodies. The exercises are whole body exercises that call on every muscle. If you have any injuries, sore spots or impairments, be gentle and work around them for now. Later, you can use what you have learned in the self-healing exercise (page 102) and in these exercises to go into and work on those areas. If you have no impairments, do each movement to full extension and contraction.

If done with total concentration, one repetition should be enough for each exercise to maintain and incrementally increase your strength each time you do it. Since you are working with the resistance of your own body/mind, there's no need to increase resistance with weights. As you get stronger the resistance naturally increases. You can easily do one repetition of the basic extension and contraction exercises (or variations on them) in a few minutes when you arise each morning, before you go to bed at night or during free moments during your day, after sitting for a long period, for example. If you wish to get stronger faster, or if you are not sure of your total concentration, you may choose to do two or three repetitions of each exercise and repeat the exercises more often.

Once you become familiar with the process and the basic exercises, develop your own variations. Doing the same exercises each day can lead to becoming stale and retard progress.

Each exercise should be done while visualizing that you're immersed up to your chin in a thick, strong, resistant, sticky glue. This visualized glue tries to hold you in place and prevent any movement. Each move that you make should be done with your attention directed to your muscles to push or pull through this glue. Pushing and pulling through it will strengthen your entire body.

Exercise 1

He who stands on tiptoe is not steady. —**Lao Tze**

Stand erect with your spine straight and head aligned—visualize a cable attached to the top of your head and suspending your weight, your feet shoulder-width apart, hands at your sides and the bottom of your spine slightly tucked under. Breathe, center and slip into Tao space. Visualize being immersed from your feet to your chin in thick glue. If you can squat, focus on your tan tien for balance and slowly ease down into a full squat. If you cannot squat, bend your knees as much as you are able. If you cannot bend your knees deeply or squat, remain standing and leave the squat for another exercise.

Unless you have a physical impairment that prevents it, you should endeavor to include the squat portion of this exercise. If you have no impairment but simply find squats difficult to do, do the squat portion of the exercise as a separate exercise. Hold on to a pole, doorway or piece of furniture if you need to do so in the beginning. When you can do one fully concentrated squat without holding on to anything, include the squat in this exercise.

Whether you are squatting or standing with your knees deeply bent, stand slowly erect, pushing against the floor and using each muscle and muscle group—including your toes, feet, calves, thighs, back and abdominals—until you are erect with knees slightly bent. Continue in one smooth movement and reach for the ceiling with every muscle from toes to fingers, fully extending back, chest, shoulders, arms, hands and fingers. Stay balanced by retaining some focus on your tan tien. During the extension, visualize that you are pushing through the glue—thick, strong glue that resists your movements. Visualize pushing through that glue with every muscle. Breathe fully and deeply as you move.

When you reach full extension, contract each muscle group—including your fingers, hands, arms, shoulders, chest, back and abdominals. Visualize contracting every muscle through thick, resistant glue, and pull your hands back down to your sides. If you can squat, do so while visualizing resistance from the glue, then return to a standing position. Visualize the glue draining away when you complete the exercise.

If you've fully visualized the glue and fully directed attention to each muscle and muscle group in turn, you should feel a flush in each muscle with only one repetition of this exercise.

Exercise 2

Stand erect with your spine straight and slightly tucked under, head aligned, hands at your sides, and feet shoulder-width apart. Breathe, center and slip into Tao space. Visualize being immersed from foot to chin in thick glue. Raise your arms from your sides, fully extended, palms up, and bring your hands together over your head, pushing through the glue. Rotate your palms and bring them back to your sides, pushing down with your palms and fingers through the glue. Breathe fully and deeply as you move.

Raise your arms from your sides, fully extended, palms inward, to shoulder level, pushing through the glue all the way. Rotate your palms to the front and bring them together in front of your chest, arms extended, elbows slightly bent, squeezing the glue together in front of you using each finger. Turn your palms to the rear, and with arms extended, elbows slightly bent, push through the glue and try to touch your palms together behind your back.

Bring your arms back to your side, extended at shoulder level, palms down. Twist your body to the left, turning your waist as far to the left as you can. While keeping your head aligned with your spine, turn your head as far to the left as you can. Try to see over your shoulder and to your back. Repeat to the right. Lower your hands to your sides.

Repeat the exercise standing only on your left foot, and then standing only on your right foot. Visualize the glue draining away when you complete each exercise.

As in all exercises, if you've fully visualized the glue and fully directed attention to each muscle and muscle group in turn, you should feel a flush in each muscle with only one repetition of this exercise.

Exercise 3

Stand erect with your spine straight and slightly tucked under, head aligned, feet shoulder-width apart and hands at your sides. Breathe, center and slip into Tao space. Visualize being immersed from foot to chin in thick glue. Raise your arms from your sides, fully extended, palms down, and bring your hands together over your head, pushing through the glue. Remember to breathe fully and deeply as you move.

While raising your hands over your head, rotate your palms to face each other, twist your body from the waist, turning as far as you can to the left and bending down to touch the floor, or if you can't touch the floor, bending down as close to the floor as possible. Visualize picking up a rock from the floor with both hands. *Keeping your hands together and holding the rock, lift the rock over your head, twisting to the right as far as you can reach. When you reach maximum extension, release the rock as if you were throwing it as far as possible.*

Return your hands to a center position over your head and repeat, twisting and bending to the right this time, and bending down to reach as close to the floor as possible. Visualize picking up another large rock with both hands. Holding the rock, lift it over your head, twisting to the left as far as you can reach. When you reach maximum extension, release the rock as if you were throwing it as far as possible.

Return your hands to center above your head. Bend forward at the waist and reach as close to the floor as possible. Once again visualize picking up a rock with both hands. Keeping your hands together and holding the rock, lift the rock over your head, leaning to the rear and throwing the rock as far behind you as possible. Repeat one more time, throwing the rock as far in front of you as possible. Visualize the glue draining away when you complete the exercise.

If you've fully visualized the glue and directed full attention to each muscle and muscle group in turn, you should feel a flush in each muscle with only one repetition of this exercise.

MOVEMENT AND PERSONAL VARIATIONS

Everyone with passing familiarity with martial arts, or even martial arts movies, has seen practitioners of Kung Fu, Karate and other martial arts move through routines where they appear to be fighting imaginary opponents. These sequences of movements are, in Kung Fu, called forms. To gain real fighting expertise, martial artists must also train in contact with real opponents. However, learning forms is of immense value in that they encode into muscle memory certain movements and ways of moving. They are also, done correctly, excellent whole body exercises.

It's beyond the scope of this book to teach formal forms, or any martial art. But by combining the visualizations in the preceding exercises and what you previously learned about walking while centered around your tan tien, you can develop your own variations on these exercises. Any movements—jumping, turning, twisting, dancing, yoga postures, throwing a basketball—can be, and should be, adapted and used as concentrated muscle extension and contraction exercises. They will all be of benefit. You can even do variations of extension and contraction exercises when bedridden due to illness or injury.

Avoid a fixed daily routine of the same exercises. Set aside a little time each day, but vary the exercises. You can also do small extension and contraction exercises, squeezing visualized rubber balls, curling your toes and picking up visualized marbles or pinching visualized coins between your fingertips.

After you've done all the exercises and some of your own for a week or so, do a repetition at top speed. Alternating slow movements at maximum strength and fast movements, still with strength, will aid in developing speed and power in your movements and also provide an aerobic benefit.

The extension and contraction exercises are foundational and will generate proportionally high returns in fitness for the time invested. With a sound foundation you can build a stronger structure. Some very advanced Chinese martial artists and fighters work at these exercises for hours each day.

BODY WEIGHT EXERCISES

Body weight exercises require you to work against physical resistance. They pump blood and oxygen through your muscles and organs, build endurance, aid coordination and build strength. Push-ups, pull-ups, squats and sit-ups (or crunches) are excellent strength and conditioning body weight exercises, as are many others. Each of these four basic exercises uses large muscle groups. Isolation exercises that only work one muscle are useful for recovering from injuries, or if you're a bodybuilder, but do not build coordination and are not especially important for the person whose primary goal is to be a survivor.

These basic four body weight exercises are important to overall fitness. If you do not know how to do them with correct form, seek out someone who does and have them show you how to do them. These exercises are so common it should be easy to find a person who knows correct form.

Body weight exercises are especially effective if done as mind/body exercises, with similar visualizations and directed attention as in the concentrated muscle extension and contraction exercises. Ten push-ups done with fully directed attention and visualizations will be of more benefit than a hundred done with scattered attention or while listening to music. You will make the most progress if you do a few concentrated repetitions with good form in each set, rather than many without attention. A set is how many repetitions you can do without resting. After resting, you may choose to do another set.

Start at whatever level of fitness you are at currently. If you cannot do one full repetition of each exercise, start by doing partials. For push-ups, start by doing one on your knees, and as you gain strength, progress to a full push-up on the balls of your feet and palms, then progress to doing them on toes and fingers. As you progress further, add concentrated repetitions and sets, and raise your feet off the ground—on a stool, chair, log or whatever is available.

If you cannot do a pull-up, stand on a chair or other object so that the bar is at chest level, grasp the bar firmly and with fully directed attention to your entire body, not just your arms, slowly lower yourself until your arms are extended. In effect, you are doing the second part of a pull-up. Continue to lower yourself, and as you progress try to do a pull-up, even a partial one. If needed, partially support your weight by standing on the chair or other object as you work towards doing your first pull-up. Continue lowering yourself from the bar until you can do one pull-up and proceed from there. If you do not have a bar available, use a tree limb or anything that will serve, such as the top of a wall or door.

If you cannot do one sit-up, start in the up position and lower your body to the floor, with attention fully directed to your body and muscles. Repeat until you can do one sit-up and continue.

If you cannot do a full squat, begin by holding onto the back of a chair or couch, a pole or a doorframe—anything that will hold your weight. Grasp the support firmly and support part of your body weight with your arms and hands.

After you can do, say, ten fully concentrated repetitions of each of these exercises with good form, try doing the next set faster while maintaining concentration. Speeding up body weight exercises provides an aerobic benefit, as well as increasing strength. As in the previous exercises, vary the repetitions, sets and frequency. Do not sacrifice form and full attention for speed, and do not fall into a fixed routine.

Note that none of these exercises require any specialized equipment. Resistance exercises using barbells and other specialized equipment have their place, if you have access to them and choose to use them. But equipment is not always available, especially if you're traveling or in the wilderness or an extended survival situation. A survivor should always be as fit as possible. If your goal is survivor-level fitness and you choose to use barbells or specialized exercise equipment, focus on major muscle group exercises and be careful to not overwork your body. Do not allow resistance exercises with weights to replace your body weight exercises or, most importantly, your concentrated extension and contraction exercises. Unless you have a purpose beyond survival conditioning, think of exercise with specialized equipment as a supplement to your daily routine. In any event, if you do use such equipment, do so with fully directed attention and visualizations.

Strong muscles without coordination, flexibility and agility are of limited use to a survivor. Better than formal routines with barbells and gym equipment is to vary your workouts and make them part of your daily life. Carry a pile of cement blocks from one side of your yard to the other; pick up one end of your couch a few times; carry heavy boxes; throw heavy and light rocks and sticks; put a rope over your shoulder and drag heavy things tied to it; do squats with full suitcases in each hand, lifting the suitcases from the floor as you squat. Make up your own variations. Always, whatever the work or exercise, do it with fully directed attention.

WALKING AND RUNNING

A good walker leaves no tracks. —**Lao Tze**

If you can't run, walk. Walk long distances. Walk fast and slow. Walk every day. Walk softly, fully centered and balanced. Do not slam your heels down. Wear comfortable shoes, preferably without heels (more to come about shoes with heels). As you walk, move from side to side, jump over small objects. Walk up and down hills. Sometimes carry a bag or a pack when you walk, your ready bag for example (more about ready bags in a later section). Everything that follows regarding running also applies to walking. Most important is to "walk lightly."

If you *can* run, run often and long, fast and slow. If you can't run now, and if at all possible and not physically hindered, get in condition by walking first, then run. Running will condition your body, help you to keep your weight at the right level, and might save your life. Cars and other forms of motorized transport are not always available and you might need to run to survive one day—many have needed to do so. If you have no transport and can't run, you can't get away from trouble quickly, run to a trouble spot to help a loved one or run for help.

Whether walking or running, practice "aimless wandering." Rather than circling a track like a caged hamster, or timing your pace and distance, simply wander about in whatever pleasant areas you can find, at whatever speed is comfortable for you. Do this in relaxed Tao space, letting intruding thoughts drift away on the air currents behind you. Only think about where you are, seeing everything around you, and where you might go next: "Oh, that trail looks interesting," or, "What's around that corner?" Stay in the moment and flow with the ground and how your body feels. This is an ancient Taoist exercise that has little in common with what our culture considers "exercise," which is mostly unpleasant and follows the "no pain, no gain" philosophy. From the Taoist point of view, if there's pain in exercise you're doing something wrong.

Our bodies have evolved to walk and run. There's nothing physical that humans do better than walk and run. Persistent hunters can run down any four-legged animal on the planet, and did so for millennia to feed their families and tribes. There are a thousand books on running. I recommend one in the "Suggested Reading" section, *Born to Run,* because it's a good story—the story of how the author discovered a way of running that is easy, natural and does not lead to injury. The way that native and first peoples the world over run. A method that is in essence Taoist.

But you don't need a book to run. Follow these instructions, stay aware and focused and you can trust your own mind/body and its feelings and judgment. You certainly do not need, and do not want, so-called running shoes with a built-up heel and "motion control" construction that prevents the natural flexion and movements of your feet. Such shoes throw you off-balance, shorten your tendons and calves, weaken your feet and with time wreck your knees and back. You might be afraid to run because you've heard or read about runners with injuries, usually damaged knees from "all that pounding." Those damaged knees and other injuries are due to overbuilt shoes and improper running methods. Runners ran in simple flats until the development a few decades ago of the raised-heel running shoes, and had fewer injuries.

These statements are supported by research done by Daniel E. Lieberman and associates at Harvard University's Skeletal Biology Lab; Dr. Craig Richards, a researcher at the University of Newcastle in Australia; Dr. Bernard Marti, the leading preventative medicine specialist at Switzerland's University of Bern; Dr. Steven Robbins and Dr. Edward Waked of McGill University in Montreal; and many others.

Get a simple, flat shoe to run or walk in. In fact, all your shoes should be flat unless you have some specialized need, ride a horse or just have to wear those Jimmy Choo spikes to the opening. Heels on boots were first designed to prevent horse riders' feet from slipping through stirrups. Then townsmen who wanted to appear as if they owned horses had heels put on their shoes. The fashion spread. Everyone had to have heels. Two hundred years later, we've forgotten why heels are on most shoes. They're for fashion, not function.

If you are accustomed to heels, you will almost certainly need a transition period to allow the muscles and tendons of your legs and feet to stretch to their natural length and to strengthen. Direct your attention to your body, especially to your feet, ankles, calves, knees and hips, as you transition from heeled shoes. Go slowly and with full awareness. Allow your tendons and muscles to develop at a comfortable pace. Do not rush, as injury might result.

Run softly and lightly with knees bent and body relaxed, fully centered around your tan tien, head aligned, tailbone tucked. Land on your midfoot, not on your heel. When running, place your foot as you did when walking in Tao space, rolling gently from midfoot to toes. Do not land with straight knees and on your heels. Your knees and feet have evolved to function as shock absorbers and they do that job very, very well—if you allow them to.

Run with directed attention and note how your body feels. Your legs should feel like springy shock absorbers when your feet strike the ground. If you're running with good form your head should not bob up and down. If you get into running at any level, you'll probably want to learn more about it. There are now thousands of people turning to running naturally, some barefoot. The Internet has many sites devoted to running barefoot, which is fine if you want to do that. But you can run free and easy in simple slippers, moccasins or other flat shoes—no need to go barefoot unless you want to do so. Trust your own judgment and body knowledge.

Bring the same level of directed attention to running that you have to the other exercises in this book. Do not run mindlessly, head down, shoulders hunched and suffering, as we see so many joggers doing. Do not run with an iPod or any kind of earphones plugged in. Do not run to music. Be present and run with your attention fully engaged. Until you are familiar with running properly to the point it becomes automatic, direct your attention to your body and run in a secure area, such as a track. Pay attention to how your feet touch the ground. Are you centered? Is your body aligned? Does some part of your body hurt? Do you need to stop and check to make sure you're not injuring yourself?

As soon as you can, get off the track and out in the world. Extend your awareness all around you as you run. "Runner's high" is real, the result of endorphins. Run for a while and you'll get it and enjoy it. Your body, brain and spirit want to run. In your early experiences of running, your mind/body might complain about the unaccustomed activity. If you're not injuring yourself, let those complaints go. Just note them and let them drift away, bubbles on the wind. When you bog down or feel like you're plodding, breathe, center if you've lost center, slip back into Tao space and visualize yourself as fleet footed, sailing along barely touching the ground. Do not concern yourself with timing your distance and speed unless you want to compete. Run easy. After you become accustomed to running while fully centered, simply run as far and as fast or slow as your mind/body tells you to. Do not exhaust yourself. Alternate running and walking as you feel you should. Running can cause the legs to stiffen if not balanced with other exercise. Be sure to continue your other exercises. Massaging your legs after running will help flexibility and ease any discomfort.

Vary your running and walking. Do not settle into a fixed routine. Run and walk hills—sand hills if you can find them. Run (or walk if you need to) stairs at a stadium, through parks, on grass and beaches. It's good conditioning to load a small backpack with water and a few odds and ends, with a total weight no more than ten pounds, and run/walk a long distance after you've worked up to it. If you want or need to train harder, load up a pack with more weight and run/walk with it. When I was younger I often ran hills with a fifty-pound pack, other times with a heavy weight in each hand, swinging them as I ran, but always retaining balance and center. Practice running often with your ready bag. You might have to do so one day.

A business associate once escaped a mugger with a knife on the street in Washington, D.C. When confronted, he quickly spun around and ran away from him. The mugger tried to catch him but could not—even though the mugger was a much younger man and my friend was running with his leather briefcase—which was also his ready bag.

I used to run and walk in the New Territories in Hong Kong with a Taoist adept, Lao Chung Li, and in other places when we went traveling. We both ran and walked in those Chinese cloth shoes you can get in any Chinatown and at martial arts supply stores—the ones with cloth soles, not the ones with hard, stiff composition soles. A local woman sewed soft rubber soles over the cloth soles for us. Chung Li ran and walked with an easy pace—sometimes fast, sometimes slow—varying his pace up and down hills. He ran with knees bent, smoothly, stepping softly and lightly and always balanced. When we weren't walking and running to a particular destination, he would dart from one side of the path to the other, jump high over small rocks, spin and run in the opposite direction, then reverse and continue in the original direction. I followed him. When out for exercise, we usually continued for about an hour or so, on occasion for most of a day, sometimes with shoulder bags with water, a snack and a few other things. "Always run and walk lightly, lightly. With the flow of the land and always with the Tao," Chung Li told me.

Survivors run.

AGILITY

Survivors are also agile. With the exception of those who are lucky enough to be carried to safety, virtually all survivors of disasters such as fires in buildings and airplanes are agile. Agility is the ability to change the body's position efficiently and requires a combination of balance, coordination, speed and reflexes. The best way to develop agility is to run impromptu obstacle courses. Jump over bushes, climb walls and trees, swing from limbs and hanging ropes, vault over dumpsters, slide under park benches. Sometimes do these things with a backpack or shoulder bag—your ready bag is best. Always do them fully centered and with directed attention.

When my sons were little, I sometimes ran a few miles with one of them on my shoulders, jumping obstacles, making quick turns, up and down hills. Other times I'd pick up two of them, one under each arm, and run up and down stairs. Every now and then, with her cooperation, I'd carry my wife in my arms and over my shoulders and run a mile or so. I did these things because I wanted to be sure I could do them in an emergency. You might want to do something similar.

SWIMMING

You can swim, right? If not, get competent instruction and learn the basic strokes. Apply the methods you've been learning to swimming—Tao space, directed attention, visualization—and you'll soon become a competent swimmer. Smooth your strokes and visualize slipping through the water like a dolphin and you'll become a good swimmer. After you become a good swimmer, learn lifesaving skills so that you can help others at need. Don't drown because you can't swim. Seventy percent of our world's surface is covered by water. Survivors can swim.

ENDURANCE AND STAMINA

Thoughts are powerful. Thoughts help to create our individual realities. Believe you can survive, or that you cannot, and you'll be correct either way. Endurance is partially physical and mostly mental.

During intense military training I saw many outstanding high school and college athletes fold up when confronted with day after day and night after sleepless night of extreme physical demands: hundreds of push-ups and other exercises daily, running constantly mile after mile, carrying each other and heavy equipment while crawling in deep sand. There was also harassment and disorientation caused by being sprayed with water and dumped into a sand pit at 3:00 in the morning, where we had to fight our way out through a wall of instructors and a tear gas cloud, with strobe lights as the only illumination, and mobs of seemingly insane people screaming at us and abusing us. Few were stopped by physical limitations, and those who were had the opportunity to get in better shape, heal from injuries or illness and try again. Few of the quitters tried again. Virtually all who quit did so because their mind told them to quit, not because their body had failed. Survivors banish failure and the concept of quitting from their world. They do not see failure or imagine quitting, and both possibilities simply cease to exist.

Stamina is a physical attribute and can be built by conditioning. Do the exercises in this book, including running and swimming if possible, or long, fast walks if you can do neither, and you'll develop stamina. If you would like to develop *more* stamina, extend the duration of the exercises and increase the quantity.

If you started at the beginning of this book and have worked your way through all of the exercises, you will have learned that you can do things that many think are not doable. Endurance is primarily a mental attribute built by enduring. But by building on skills you have developed from previous exercises in this book, there's a way to improve endurance without first enduring survival conditions.

Exercise

Think of a difficult task. For example, descending a mountain carrying a fellow climber with a broken leg, or running ten miles carrying five gallons of water to your family stranded in the desert—after you've missed a night's sleep, a couple of meals and with a broken rib or three. Make it a task that would matter a great deal to you, perhaps a life-or-death situation. Using the same tools of directed attention and visualization, make it your fully committed intention to save your friend or family, and see yourself successfully accomplishing the task. See yourself doing the task step-by-step. Do not focus only on the goal. Feel the sweat, the sore feet, the aching lungs, the shortness of breath and pain from your injury, and see yourself leaving all that behind and continuing to run. Then visualize a wolf pack chasing you and run faster.

As you will learn how to do in the exercises in the "Managing Pain" section (page 100), let pain wash through you. Feel cramps in your side and let them wash through you and dissipate. Feel the pain of sharp stones under your bare feet, and branches whipping your face as you run through a visualized forest, and let the pain wash through you and keep on running.

If you *see* and *feel* yourself doing these things with fully directed attention and belief, you're almost there. Now all you have to do is *do* it, if the situation arises. And do some actual physical training, because at some point you have to do the training, not just read about it. The mind/body exercises, visualization and directed attention go a long way towards preparing you, but not all the way. Set up scenarios similar to those you have visualized and do them as part of your training. Don't only train on nice days and when it's comfortable and you're in the mood. Survival situations don't always arise on sunny days when you're in top condition and ready to rock. You can't select a time when you'll be faced with a survival situation. If you could, you could arrange to not be there.

At one point in my personal training I used to go outside at night in winter with snow and ice on the ground, barefoot and clad only in running shorts, and fight full contact with two of my training partners. They wore boots and warm clothing. That may sound tough, but it was nothing—just training. I was in Tao space and with the Tao. Do not train *hard*. Train easy. Stay loose. Go with the flow, with the Tao.

PHYSICAL LIMITATIONS

About 50 percent of the general population has some kind of physical limitation. Some are minor, some severe. Most can be overcome in order to survive. With the right attitude you can work around physical limitations that many regard as crippling. We've all seen sporting events in which people in wheelchairs and prosthetics compete. Many of us have known people who overcame their physical limitations to lead not only a regular life, but an exceptional one.

Many of the martial arts schools I've trained in had students with severe physical limitations. One person in particular I remember was a man who was a paraplegic. He had a light wheelchair in which he could spin and move as fast as most students with functioning legs could move. He trained with the rest of the students and demanded that no one make exceptions for him. This was a hard, full-contact school. There were times when he was kicked out of his chair and onto the concrete floor we trained on. He could move across the floor, pulling himself quickly to the legs of his attacker, and bring him down to the floor and choke him out as fast or faster than many who were fully enabled. He was a formidable opponent. He told me he had once been robbed and beaten before he had started training in martial arts, and had decided that was never going to happen to him again; that if he was attacked again he was going to fight. He might lose, but he was going to be nobody's victim.

In my Jump School class there was a student who was much older than the rest of us, a veteran of the Korean War. He had been bayoneted through the left lung. Under stress, that lung would partially collapse. Jump School was constant stress. When his lung started to collapse, which it did during long runs, he would hunch to one side, pound his elbow into his ribs, suck in as much air as he could and get his lung working again. His presence and quiet fortitude gave courage to some who were thinking about quitting and shamed those who did quit.

An old friend and former business partner has had severe limitations from birth. A detailed list of his bodily misfunctions and the constant pain he has to deal with would be the size of a menu in a Chinese restaurant. Yet I worked with him for months before I learned about his limitations. One sweltering July day he walked with me for miles in Manhattan's concrete canyons. There were no cabs to be had. It was only when he turned pale, broke out in a heavy sweat and was clearly in great pain that he said he needed to "sit and rest for a minute." He has persevered through many surgeries, much pain, recurring illnesses and at least two near-death experiences with good humor. In twenty years I've never seen him feel sorry for himself, make excuses or do anything but perform at the top of his abilities. He's one of the bravest persons I've ever known, an inspiration and a survivor.

You have a physical limitation that might affect your ability to survive? Work around it. Survive and live life fully.

Sometimes breathing is hard, sometimes it comes easily;
Sometimes there is strength and sometimes weakness.
—Lao Tze

CONTROLLING YOUR BIOCHEMISTRY AND MIND/BODY STATES

HEAT AND COLD

You've probably read or heard stories about monks in the Himalayas who can sit for hours in a snowdrift and not only stay warm but also melt the snow around them. Those stories are true. And no, it's not magic. If you've done all the lessons in this book so far, you can probably figure out how those monks do this, and how you also can. Tao space, directed attention and visualization enable you to control body temperature, as they enable you to contrail pain and heal illness.

Suppose you're camping in the woods and a quick cold snap comes in. Your clothing and sleeping bag are inadequate. You're cold. Of course you're going to build a fire, if you can. While building your fire, or if the fire goes out, or if you can't start a fire, you might want to generate some internal heat. You can generate body heat by physical exercise, but that gets tiring pretty fast. Internal heat, which can last much longer and which expends far less energy, can be generated by using methods you've learned in this book.

Exercise 1

To generate internal heat, sit or stand comfortably, slip into Tao space and direct your attention into your body. See and feel your entire body from the top of your head to the tips of your toes. Visualize your tan tien as a ball of comfortable warmth. See and feel it radiating the kind of warmth a potbellied stove gives off in a log cabin. As you breathe in and down to your tan tien, visualize your tan tien converting your breath to heat, the same way a stove draws in air to fuel its fire. As you breathe out, see and feel that heat radiate from your tan tien throughout your body, warming your belly and chest and moving inside your arms and legs to your fingers and toes to warm them.

Do this exercise on a cold, or at least cool, day. Remember to remain relaxed and in Tao space. With clear visualization and feeling you will feel heat rising from your tan tien fairly quickly. As in other exercises, if for any reason you don't have success on your first effort, repeat the exercise until you do.

Exercise 2

Reverse the visualizations and feelings to cool your body in hot weather. Breathe in and see and feel the air coming into your tan tien as fresh, cool mountain air. As it reaches your tan tien it becomes a ball of refreshing coolness. As you breathe out see and feel that coolness radiate from your tan tien throughout your body, cooling your belly and chest and moving inside your arms and legs to your fingers and toes to cool them.

Of course you should do the obvious things if you get overheated on a hot, sunny day: cover up, get into the shade, drink plenty of water. Do not abuse your skills by sitting in the hot sun and not sweating to show off to friends.

To develop expertise, practice heating or cooling your body whenever the local weather gets uncomfortable. You might find that with a little effort you can be comfortable in weather that previously made you miserably hot or shivering with cold. In a survival situation, say if you're stuck in the desert or mountains, these skills can be invaluable and might save your life. But understand and remember that you're using energy, physical energy, to generate these mind/body states. In normal circumstances you might find that you can manage heat or cold well enough to make yourself comfortable with little effort. In extreme situations, however, most of us can only sustain these states for limited periods. Doing any of the extension and contraction exercises at very low intensity, or sitting, standing and walking in Tao space while visualizing and feeling energy being drawn into your body, will extend your ability to maintain mind/body states. Advanced adepts can sustain these mind/body states for extended periods in extreme conditions without food. The rest of us must at some point replenish the expended energy with food.

BEING UNSEEN OR SEEN

I once had a student who was a famous rock-and-roll performer at the height of her popularity. When she was on stage she commanded the attention of thousands. She was beautiful, electric, sexy, bigger than life. Sometimes when she walked into a crowd at a private party she drew everyone's attention to her entrance. Other times not. When we walked down the street to a café after her lesson no one noticed her. On stage she was always "on." When making an entrance she was sometimes on, sometimes off, depending on the crowd and her mood. Off-stage, if she chose to be, she was off, and could become almost invisible. In certain agencies, covert operators are taught to "go gray" or become "gray men" to escape the notice of others. In Taoist training a few students are taught to become "unseen." There are some commonalities in all three abilities.

The covert operator is taught to wear clothing that blends with what others are wearing, to behave discreetly and to not draw attention. Performing artists learn to dress down if they don't want to be noticed off-stage and to change their body language in subtle ways: slumping slightly, not making direct eye contact, moving with the slightest hesitation. Most importantly, they draw in the energy that onstage or on-screen they project so powerfully. Watch any skilled actor in a film and you'll see him or her shift personas and/or develop their character. Note how the actor's body language changes while developing or shifting personas. You don't have to be a film actor to shift personas. Most of us do this to a certain extent whether we're conscious of it or not. Do you occupy the same persona at work and at home playing with your children?

Obviously being able to become unseen could be a critical survival skill. Being able to project energy at will is also a useful skill. Taoist training in being not seen focuses on energy management and teaches a method of being on or off that is highly effective. An adept can become almost invisible. Any skilled practitioner can retract their energy enough to be able to slip past a potentially hostile crowd, or project it enough to, say, impress a ticket agent to give them the last seat on a plane leaving a war zone in a country where civil war has broken out.

In Hong Kong, one of my teachers always entered the training hall with an erect posture and eyes flashing—a striking, charismatic man striding energetically to the head of the class projecting a bubble of energy strong enough to break windows. One day while walking down Nathan Road, the main artery of Kowloon, I spotted this teacher as he passed me. His posture was relaxed and balanced. His energy was not noticeable. He blended with the crowd and was completely forgettable. He quickly looked at me when I spotted him and said, "Ha. You can see pretty good. No one else see me." Although he had changed his posture for the street, and pulled in his energy, his alertness and ability to feel the energy of others when directed at him was as acute as when he was "on," a showbiz term he was not familiar with but recognized at once when I used it. "Yes," he said. "On and off. Good way to describe. Can turn on and off as you want."

The external ways of being unseen are to dress to blend in and to adjust your body language. The internal way is to manage your energy. Do the following exercise a few times and you'll learn to switch on and off in a split second. Given that you've done all the lessons leading up to this, you should find this relatively easy to accomplish.

Exercise

Slip into Tao space. Visualize the electromagnetic energy that radiates around your body as a bubble. When you want to be unnoticed, see the energy bubble contracting around your body. Bring it in until it's as close to you as a tight garment. To project energy, reverse the process. Visualize your energy bubble filling with energy and expanding. You might want to initiate the process by thinking, "switch on and expand, or switch off and contract."

Practice entering rooms and walking in crowded places in off mode and in on mode and observe people's reactions to your presence. See how close you can come to someone who knows you while in off mode without them noticing you. Do not tiptoe or sneak. Simply walk close to them and wait for them to notice you. If they say, "I didn't see you standing there," you've learned to be off. Reverse the process and walk into a room filled with people, or a store or café where you're meeting a friend. If everyone looks at you, or if your friend says, "You look like you own the place," you've learned to be on.

MANAGING PAIN

All of us experience pain in our lives, both physical and emotional. It's part of the human condition. In a survival situation, or in everyday life (which in fact *is* a survival situation), physical pain can be debilitating and affect our ability to function. So can emotional pain, but that's a subject for another book.

There's an ancient Taoist saying that has passed into Chan and Zen: "Pain inevitable. Suffering optional." This aphorism refers to much more than physical pain management and edges into philosophical areas. But it's a good thing to remember when you're in physical pain and applying the pain management technique you are about to learn. Being able to manage severe pain might save your life.

Suppose you're cooking dinner on your little backpacker's stove and your hiking companion knocks the stove over, spilling a pot of boiling water on your feet. You leap up, run to the stream and put your feet in the cool, fast-running water. The stream water helps a little to reduce the cantaloupe-sized blisters on the top of your feet, and helps soothe the excruciating pain a little. Very little. You're sweating and shaking and experiencing severe debilitating pain, like a twenty on a scale of ten. Ask any burn victim: nothing is more painful than a bad burn. You realize you've got third-degree burns and you know they're already infected—third-degree burns always get infected. Your companion offers to go for help and try to find some rescue people to carry you out. You're in a deep, narrow canyon. No way a helicopter or jeep can get in. When and if help is found, they'll have to walk in. You're ten rough miles from the trailhead where your car is parked and night is falling quickly. Your companion can't see in the dark and wants to wait till morning to go for help. After climbing out of the canyon, finding help and getting back to the trailhead it will be nightfall tomorrow at the earliest, probably much later. Your companion is not an experienced woodsman, is unsure on the trail and has no idea where to go for help—and might get lost simply trying to find the trailhead. Assuming a rescue organization is found, most likely the rescue people will want to wait for daylight to come in. Then it'll take them all day to get in—if your companion remembers the way back to the camp. It's highly questionable whether they'll reach you within forty-eight hours. It could easily take three to four days before medical help with antibiotics reaches you. By that time your feet would be so infected a surgeon might have to take them off, if you survive the systemic infection. What do you do?

Using the pain management methods you're about to learn, you break and drain the blisters, wrap your feet in bandages, cut the tops from your sneakers to allow room for your grotesquely swollen feet and using night-vision methods walk out that night, leading your companion. You reach medical care in early morning, about fifteen hours after the accident. They pump you full of antibiotics and schedule you for skin grafts. You get to keep your feet. And your life.

This did happen to an experienced woodsman, exactly as described. Note that he also used other skills taught in this book, such as night vision and centered decision-making. There's another chapter to this story; it's in the next section on self-healing. For now, let's learn how to manage pain.

SEEING PAIN

It's very difficult for this exercise to be effective unless you have some actual pain to work with. You can use remembered and visualized pain as an aid, but doing so adds a layer of visualization and makes it all too easy to imagine that you've learned to deal with actual physical pain when you've only mastered visualized pain. It's best to begin by dealing with irritations such as mosquito bites and pain from minor injuries such as a small cut or burn you might get in the kitchen. Read through the exercise and remember it, and the next time you have a minor pain to deal with, refresh your memory by re-reading the exercise—then apply it. After working with lower-level pain you'll be better equipped to cope with a more serious injury or pain.

Exercise

Start by identifying the pain you want to deal with. Go into Tao space. Relax your body and direct your attention to the top of your head and into your brain. Visualize your brain, then move your attention downwards to your spine where it begins at the base of your skull. Follow your spine with your directed attention all the way to your sacrum. Feel and visualize the bones, the joints, the interior of your spine. See it as clearly as you can see your hand when your eyes are open.

Now go back to the top of your head and focus your attention on the neural network that connects your entire body. Visualize the nerves running from the base of your skull, down your spine, radiating out from your spine through your torso and through your arms and legs. Stay with this as long as it takes to visualize your nerves, the transmission system of sensation in your body. Do not forget to breathe deeply and slowly and to stay in Tao space.

Notice that the nerves where you are experiencing what we call pain are radiating a different kind of energy than in the areas where you do not feel the pain. Closely visualize the nerves in this area. See the traceries of filaments. Visualize the actual nerve impulses as they flow up your spine and to your brain. See these nerve impulses as a stream of hot red energy.

Do not name that energy stream as pain. Pain is nothing more than a label we put on certain nerve impulses. Naming it as pain causes us to tighten up and resist it, which intensifies the feelings. Allow it to become an unnamed sensation.

Refine your attention further and go into the nerve impulse stream. Trace it from its beginnings through your system of nerves into and up your spine and to your brain. Do not resist this unnamed, hot, red-colored sensation. Simply be with it. See it. Feel it. Feel it as being hotter than the other portions of your nerve stream. Become familiar with it, with its heat and red color. Recognize it as part of you, a part of you that is as much yours as your arms, a part that can be moved and directed as easily as your arms.

TRANSFORMING SENSATIONS

In recent years, pain management by various visualization methods has entered into mainstream Western medicine and is taught to those who suffer from chronic pain. This particular visualization is a contemporary update of a centuries-old Taoist method, and differs from simple visualization in that it activates chi, or body energy.

Exercise

While still in Tao space, visualize a tiny trickle of cool blue energy flowing slow-ly down from your brain through your spine, spreading though your neural net-work and into the location with the hot red sensations. Visualize this energy as cool blue water. Feel the cool blue water flowing and spreading into and through all the tributaries in your entire system of nerves and into the hot red area. Focus on feeling this water, like you feel a drink of ice water on a hot summer day. Feel it as it spreads internally and cools your nerves, as that ice water cooled your mouth, throat and stomach. As the cool blue water encounters the hot red energy flow, the water transforms it into cool blue water. There is no battle, no struggle, no fighting one with the other, no conflict or difficulty. The hot red stream is tired and wants to relax and change its nature and become calm, cool and blue, and be in harmony and balance with the rest of the system it is a part of. Direct the cool blue water flow to continue through your body and wash out through the soles of your feet. This stream of cool blue water is never-ending. Its source is constantly renewed. The stream will continue to flow as long as you want or need it to.

Don't forget to breathe deeply, to remain relaxed. Do not tense when you encounter hot red energy. Let it flow until the cool blue energy reaches it and transforms it. If you're dealing with chronic pain you'll probably find that you'll *need to repeat this process from time to time. Nothing in life is permanent. With practice you can learn to transform hot red energy (pain) into a cool blue flow in less than a minute.*

When the pain has washed through you and out of your body, take a deep breath and withdraw your attention.

SELF-HEALING

I once asked a Taoist adept, who was a master of healing, what he would do if he got shot or hit by a car. Would he treat himself or seek medical attention? He looked at me as if he had suddenly discovered I was deficient in intelligence and said, "Am I an idiot? I would go to the emergency room and let the doctors do what they do. And I would use all my power to help heal myself." This is exactly what the man with burned feet did. More on that after we learn the basic healing process.

These skills do not replace professional medical attention for serious injuries or illness—unless there's none available, in which case you might have to rely on whatever medical skills you possess and what you learn in this book. Visualization combined with energetic healing is highly effective, if applied properly. The basic process is similar to that of managing pain, one exception being that you direct your attention to your entire body rather than only your neural network.

These processes can be done standing, sitting or lying down. It's best, if possible, to lie down on your back. The basic healing process we will learn is for the whole body, for use when you have a systemic illness. A variation, which follows, is for use on a specific injury.

Exercise

Go into Tao space. Relax your body and direct your attention to the top of your head, then move your attention downwards and through your entire body. Feel and visualize your muscles, bones and organs as you scan downwards from the top of your head to the tips of your toes. Follow your body with your directed attention. Feel and visualize all of your muscles, bones, joints and organs. See them as clearly as you can see your hand when your eyes are open. Stay with this visualization as long as it takes to see and feel your body. Do not forget to breathe deeply and slowly and to stay in Tao space.

See the discomfort and illness you are experiencing as being red and hot. If you're running a fever this should be quite easy. Does this red heat extend through your entire body at the same intensity, or is there a localized area where it's more intense, such as your abdomen? Whether it's everywhere equally or there is a specific location that's more intense, we start the same way.

See yourself lying on your back in a shallow stream of cool, clean, clear water in the midst of a safe and green forest. Under you the streambed is golden sand. You are comfortable here, at ease and relaxed, at home. The water that feeds this stream springs from deep under the earth and brings with it the primal healing energy of our planet. This water of the earth flows gently over and through your body, caressing and cooling it. This clean water finds its way into every part of your body, flowing through your brain, down through your throat, through your chest, down your arms and into your belly and tan tien, down and through your legs and feet. It touches and washes through every muscle fiber, the marrow in your bones, your heart and lungs and every organ in your body. As the water flows through your body it washes everything clean, and taking with it everything red and hot it flows out from your feet and into the stream, which continues on, transforming all red heat into clear, clean, cool water before it sinks back into the earth.

If you have a specific injury or area of discomfort, see the water find its own way to that particular spot. You do not need to direct the flow of this earth water. It is healing water and has the wisdom of our earth guiding its flow. Simply direct some of your attention to this spot and feel the water cooling and cleaning as it flows through.

Remain in this healing stream for as long as you like, being healed, refreshed and renewed. You are comfortable here. You are at home and can stay as long as you want, and can return whenever you choose.

When the healing water has done its work and you feel you've been in this space long enough, take a deep breath, withdraw your attention and return to your usual activities.

There are other, specific processes for specific illnesses, and a process for scanning your body and its internal workings in order to maintain good health. These are beyond the scope of this book and will be detailed in my next book, *The Tao of Health, Diet and Well-Being*.

Remember the fellow with the burned feet? He went to the Grossman Burn Center in Sherman Oaks, California, a world-famous facility. Before the burn specialist performed the skin grafts he told the injured man that grafts didn't always take, and that if they did not he would need to try again. When the burned man came up from anesthesia he began the healing process described above. He repeated these healing processes many times each day and each night, when he was awakened by nurses or by the other patients, all of whom were in intense pain. He also did specialized visualizations for this specific healing.

The doctor, world-famous burn specialist Dr. Richard Grossman, told him to expect to be in the hospital for seven to ten days, the minimum time required to make sure the grafts had taken and that he was out of danger from infection. Three days after surgery, during his daily exam, the doctor was amazed to see that the grafts had completely healed. He said this was the fastest healing he had ever witnessed, had his staff photograph the grafts and released the man the same day.

Remember, creating these mind/body states uses physical energy that must be replaced. The easiest way to do that is to eat more food. The fellow who was burned ate about 5,000 calories a day during treatment and for a week or two afterwards. Advanced adepts can draw much energy from the earth and air, but those methods are beyond the scope of this book.

FEAR

Like fire, fear is a good servant and a bad master. Controlled, it can save your life. Uncontrolled, it can take it. Fear and the biochemicals it triggers can make you faster than a speeding bullet and able to leap tall buildings in a single bound. Well, not really—just checking to see if you're awake. But fear can make you stronger, faster, more agile, and able to think quickly and make the right decisions—if it's controlled and channeled. Fear can also cause you to make decisions that can disable you and turn you into a whimpering puddle, and get you killed. Survivors are not controlled by fear; they make an ally of fear, welcome its arrival and use the enhanced abilities it brings with it.

All fears, even small ones like fear of spiders and snakes, are like vines wrapped around the trunk of a tree that is our biggest fear—the fear of death. Fear of death and other fears are so closely intertwined that it's difficult to pick them apart and see them as separate things. But in order to deal with them, pick them apart we must. As we do so, we will see that all fears are rooted in fear of death. So to deal with fear and fear of death we can start with any fear. How do we make an ally of fear? We do so by not running from it. By facing it, letting it flow through us and dissipate. Face fear, let it flow through you and it will lose its power over you and become your ally.

I was once on a small aircraft about to take off when the last pas-
senger boarded and sat beside me. He was a young man, large, athletic,
sweating, red-faced and breathing heavily as if he had been running. We
buckled up and the plane taxied to the runway. He introduced himself as
Mike and asked me if I had ever flown before. I told him that I had flown
hundreds of thousands of miles all around the world. Mike said this was
his first flight and that he was so frightened he almost didn't board. He
was still breathing heavily and sweating—from fear, not running. He was
totally and helplessly in the grip of fear, almost disabling fear.

The plane took off and Mike closed the shade and looked away from
the window—he had the window seat. He continued to talk, speaking
fast and stumbling over his words, almost babbling. I told him to take a
deep breath. Mike looked at me, stopped talking for a moment and did
take a deep breath. He then asked me how I remained calm when we
could be killed if the plane crashed. We talked for a while, me trying to
calm him and encouraging him to breathe deeply. But it was apparent
that his fear was extreme. He took off his seat belt, went to the flight attendant and demanded the plane return and land. The attendant was out
of her depth and asked me to help.

I pointed out to Mike that the most dangerous portions of any flight
were takeoff and landing. Now that we were in the air we had to land,
and so might as well continue to our destination and land there. Mike
returned to his seat and again asked me how I managed to not be afraid.
He was amazed that I could sit and read as the plane took to the sky. He
continued to quiz me about my calmness and to fidget with his seat belt.
He displayed all the symptoms of a person about to give in to panic and
act irrationally. Both the attendant and I were concerned that he might
push his way into the cockpit and interfere with the pilot.

Judging that the best way to calm him and avoid having to restrain
him physically would be to help him overcome his fear, I offered to teach
him a technique that could possibly, if he committed to doing it fully,
free him from his fear. I explained to him that I was not a psychologist
or therapist of any kind and warned him that the method could be even
more difficult for him to deal with than simply being in an aircraft in
flight. He agreed to try it.

I asked him what would be the worst possible thing he could imagine happening. He said the plane crashing. I told him to sit back in his
seat, close his eyes and breathe deeply. As much as possible I wanted to
get him into Tao space. He followed my instructions, and when he was

as relaxed as he was going to get I told him to visualize the following scenario.

The plane is flying smoothly and all appears to be well. Suddenly there's a massive explosion at the front of the aircraft. Flames flare, smoke billows and a shock wave rolls over us. You feel the heat of the flames and the impact of the shock wave and smell the smoke. The front portion of the aircraft is totally blown away, right up to our row of seats. You can now see the sky through the ragged opening in front of us. You sit strapped into your seat as this part of the aircraft tips forward and begins its long fall to earth. You feel the wind rushing over you and hear the screams of the passengers behind us. You see the ground coming closer and closer as our damaged fragment of fuselage continues its fall to earth. You see everything on the ground getting larger and larger, and can now see individual houses and trees, and now it seems you are falling faster and faster, and now you can see leaves on the trees and the grass growing and the earth is getting closer. Then you hit the ground. The fuselage crashes with a crushing impact and for a split second you feel the impact and overwhelming pain, and in another split second you are crushed and everything goes black. You are now dead. This life you love so much is over. Now whatever you believe will happen does happen. Everything stays black and life is over. Or you see a light and are drawn to it. Whatever you think will happen after death, this life has come to an end. Now there's no need to fear anything.

As I talked Mike through this process, reminding him to breathe deeply and slowly, I watched him closely to make sure this exercise was not too much for him. If it had been, I would have stopped and diverted to another exercise. But Mike stayed with the exercise. I watched him twitch and squirm. His closed eyes rolled and moved back and forth under his eyelids. He continued to sweat heavily. He displayed all the symptoms of a person in extreme distress—until the plane crashed. When he experienced the crash and his death he at once grew calm and stopped squirming and sweating.

I told him to take another deep breath, exhale fully and open his eyes. When he did so, he looked at me with astonishment and smiled. "That's it," he said. "The worst thing that can happen is that I die. I'm going to die anyway sometime. Well, what the hell. That's all there is?" We talked about the process and I advised him how to use it for other things. As we talked, the plane landed, with Mike looking out the window and enjoying the view. After landing we walked together into the terminal. Mike bounced along a foot off the ground, smiling, relaxed, happy.

I would not have attempted such instruction under such stressful circumstances if doing so had not seemed like the lesser risk. There was a real possibility that Mike would have not been able to handle this fear management method and would have become even more fearful and possibly unruly. However, Mike was on the verge of total panic and had already left his seat once and made irrational demands of the attendant. If Mike had rushed into the cockpit and interfered with the pilot, which the attendant and I were trying to avert, he could have caused the plane to crash. I was prepared to restrain him physically, but the possibility of a tussle on a small aircraft seemed to be the greater risk. In this instance, all turned out well. Do not try to do this sort of thing yourself. If you are not fully competent to teach these methods, and to evaluate your students both before the process and during it, and if you are not prepared to deal with possible negative outcomes, do not even attempt to teach these methods to another person.

The example I cited with Mike in the aircraft is the process by which you can overcome any fear—if you are prepared for possible consequences and willing to deal with possible emotional stress. I used this example to get your attention and to illustrate how effective this method can be. However, it's best to start with a small fear rather than a disabling one. Are you afraid of snakes but not terrified of them? If so, that might be a good place to start.

Exercise

Slip into Tao space, something at which you are now fully accomplished. Visualize your fear, whatever it may be, and go directly into it. Take it to its conclusion. Face the fear, go through it and let it all wash through you and away.

When you do visualizations of fear-producing situations, do them with full engagement as you have in previous exercises. As you center and enter Tao space, engage your senses and feel the bodily sensations of fear, the flow of adrenalin that produces quickened breath, increased pulse rate and heightened sensitivity. As those bodily sensations occur, slow your breathing and calmly face your fear while allowing those bodily sensations to become familiar to you. Accept the physical effects of fear as simply another state of being, like experiencing heat or cold. You might think of the arrival of these sensations as an internal wave of adrenalin, one you're riding and using to your benefit.

As you can see, dealing with Mike's fear led him at once to the root of all fear: fear of death. Other fears may be more entangled with each other and might require you to pick them out of the thicket of your psyche and deal with them one by one. It could be a long process, but it is one well worth doing in that it leads to a free life not governed by fear.

As additional exercises, set up actual fear-producing situations, with proper safeguards, and work your way through them. For example, fear of heights is ingrained in our species at the DNA level. To make an ally of this fear you could, after doing the visualizations, enroll in a rock climbing class with competent and safety-conscious instructors. As you climb, stay centered. When fear arrives, perhaps when you're thirty feet from the ground on a sheer rock face, you'll feel the body sensations: a surge of adrenalin so powerful your hands might shake. Welcome it. Your ally fear has arrived to help you. Feel its power flow through your body and make you stronger. Feel your reflexes quicken, your thought processes sharpen. Use fear's bodily manifestations to your benefit. You're in the Zone, in Tao space. Enjoy it. Continue to climb with your enhanced abilities. When you reach the top you'll feel a burst of exhilaration. Fear is now your ally.

SURVIVOR'S MIND AND THE TAO

SURVIVAL SITUATIONS

When most people think of survival situations they think of getting lost in the wilderness and starving, or being attacked by a mountain lion or bear or bitten by a poisonous snake. Or they think of being caught in a natural disaster such as an earthquake, hurricane, tornado or flood. In today's climate many worry about becoming a victim of a terrorist attack. Prospective international travelers worry about the cruise ship sinking, or getting malaria or being mugged by criminals in faraway places. The more imaginative among us worry about getting stung by a deadly wasp or eaten by the tiger at the zoo.

How can we possibly be prepared for all these disparate threats? Reading and learning about conditions in specific locations, and acquiring situation-specific skills for activities in which we engage is useful and appropriate. But each day in everyone's life is a survival situation. Anything can happen on any day, and often does. Sunrise does not promise sunset. And so we daily practice the mind/body skills we have learned, and we deal with our fears by facing them so that they lose their power over us. A survivor grounded in Taoist skills and philosophy greets each day fully centered, aware, ready and free from fear's disabling effects. He or she approaches each day as an adventure, which it is if we're paying attention. By daily use we continue to strengthen our foundation of survival skills so they will serve us in everyday life and in extraordinary circumstances.

There are martial arts that teach specific responses to specific acts. Someone grabs your wrist; what do you do? Someone tries to choke you from behind; what do you do? The problem with this kind of training is that you're caught with no response if your attacker does anything you have not trained for. Much better is to learn skills that can be applied in many circumstances. That is what we have done in the first part of this book. Now, rather than learning how to avoid being eaten by the tiger at the zoo or stung by a wasp, we'll build on our foundation of mind/body skills by practicing them—and by expanding concepts and knowledge.

You're at a table in a café enjoying the view, your companion and your drink. You're not thinking about what to do if a black widow spider is under the table. But if there is one there, and if it ever-so-softly lands in your lap, you'll know at once and react appropriately.

A person approaches you on the street with a story about their car being broken down and asks for help. You'll engage your perception, decide if they need help or if it feels wrong and react accordingly.

You're at an amusement park about to board a roller coaster when, because your senses are fully engaged, you notice that some of the bolts securing the track are loose. You tell the attendant. He shrugs it off. You make a split-second decision, point out the shoddy maintenance to others waiting to board, get out of line, taking your children with you, and report the situation to management.

You're in the airport waiting to board, and because you're not in traveler's coma but aware and noticing your surroundings, you see a gun under a guy's jacket and wonder if he's a cop or a bad guy. Do you run screaming for the exit, or do you pull in your energy, fade back into the crowd and go notify a security person?

You're drinking your latte and reading the news on your iPad and you notice this guy watching you. He's cute and is totally, completely, intensely focused on you. Is he checking you out? Does he think those Jimmy Choo spikes are killer or is he some kind of stalker? He gets up from his chair and comes over to you and . . . Every woman knows how to evaluate this situation and the person. Except those who don't. If you've worked through the lessons and are centered you will not be one of those who do not know. You'll direct your attention and focus your senses and perception to assess this person. What do his lifelines tell you? Who is the child inside the adult? What's his vibe, the one that's deep under his surface manner? Who is he really?

You're about to enter a mall when you get this weird feeling. You don't know why you feel strange, but for some reason you're reluctant to enter the mall. You hesitate for a second, think about it, decide to heed your feelings, return to your car and continue on your other errands. Later you hear on the radio that there was a shooting in the mall. Wow! Are you psychic? If you've been doing the lessons, you already know the answer to that question.

You're hiking on a mountain trail and come into a green and shaded glade, and suddenly you feel . . . something. Because you're fully centered and aware, you'll stop, look all around, listen, smell and extend your perception. Could there be a mountain lion hiding in the brush and waiting for a tasty hiker, or a bear intending to mug a backpacker for the freeze-dried food in the pack? You don't sense any large animals in the area. But something feels wrong. Your mind tells you this is a lovely little shaded spot, perfect for lunch. But still, you sense some kind of energy, or vibe, and don't feel welcome in this place. Maybe it's an unfriendly earth spirit. First peoples the world over believe in earth spirits, entities that inhabit a certain place. But no, you're a modern, civilized person, a child of the Enlightenment and member of a society based on scientific thought. There can't be any such thing as spirits. That's just primitive superstition. Then you remember that the Japanese, who are modern people with a scientific and technological society, believe in *kami,* which is what they call earth spirits; they even build shrines to them. Could there be such things? Maybe, maybe not. In any event you perceive something. You feel uneasy. What to do? You trust your perception and leave the glade at once.

You get the idea. Continue to practice the lessons you have learned. Not just at home during the time you do the actual lessons. Use them each day as you go about your affairs. Make them part of your life.

By being fully aware, you will know when you need to acquire situational skills and knowledge. Going to Thailand, Australia, the Philippines or Malaysia? Read about your destination. Not only tourist brochures—dig a little. The ocean in all those places is home to the box jellyfish, or sea wasp. In the Philippines, twenty to thirty people each year die from stings from these creatures; many more are envenomed and become extremely ill. I haven't seen anything mentioned in tourist brochures about this. Don't let such things prevent you from traveling. Just be aware of them and stay out of their way. Dozens of tourists have been robbed and many murdered on the streets of America. Yet we daily go about our business because we know how to avoid most dangerous situations.

Having a plan in case of a house fire or earthquake or hurricane or if the boat sinks is only prudent. But trying to plan for all eventualities is a never-ending and ultimately fruitless task. Better to have specific plans for likely events and trust yourself to react appropriately when the unexpected occurs, as it will. If you live where floods are likely, you'll have an escape route planned; if in an earthquake zone, you'll have food and water stored; if you're concerned about economic disaster, you'll have a store of cash. By living the skills you have developed you continue to develop a survivor's mind/body. When the exceptional occurs you'll be ready to deal with it and survive. Meantime, watch the sunset and enjoy life.

INTUITION AND ANALYSIS

First thought, best thought. **—Taoist saying**

This aphorism stems from the belief that intuition provides us with the best course of action in any given situation. As a general rule this is true, *if* the information you acquire is accurate and not colored by fear or preconceptions, and if you have a clear understanding of the situation and your needs.

Intuition, sometimes called instinct, operates faster than conscious reason and can trigger a physical response before a thought is fully formed. I was once walking along a trail a little way behind a friend, Rich, who was a very switched-on guy. I heard a faint buzzing sound ahead of us and instantly Rich performed a reverse standing broad jump of about twelve feet, landing on my shoes. As he jumped he said, "rrrraa . . ." When he landed he completed his thought: "Rattlesnake, that's a rattlesnake." Indeed it was. A large timber rattler that had no further interest in Rich, or me, and slithered off into the undergrowth.

If Rich had taken time to consciously analyze the situation, his mental processes might have gone something like this: "Buzzing sound. What's that? Something on the trail. Hmm, something coiled. Snake? Diamond-shaped head, which means it's a viper. Its head is raised and looking directly at me and I'm getting this queasy feeling in the pit of my stomach. I think that's a timber rattler about six feet long. Big enough to be very dangerous. I'm wearing sneakers and shorts. It could easily bite me and inject hemotoxic venom. Might kill me. Better get out of the way. Should warn James, too. *Jump.*"

If Rich had not acted on intuition he might have been bitten. A bite from that particular snake could have killed him; it certainly would have made him extremely sick and caused major tissue damage. Fortunately, Rich *did* act on his intuition, which drew information from his data bank to identify the creature and alert him to danger. All of us have this innate capacity. If we did not, we wouldn't be here; our remote ancestors wouldn't have made it off that African plain where *Homo sapiens* got started.

Unfortunately, many of us have had our acute senses and that powerful intuition blunted by modern life and lack of use. The lessons you have completed have awakened your senses to a fine degree. Now, as you go about your life and continue to keep your senses sharp, and as you acquire and update accurate information about your environment for your intuition to process, your intuition can become a more refined and reliable survival tool.

For example, as a matter of course you should note all the exits to any building and any room you enter. As you get into a vehicle you should note how many doors there are. When you buckle a seat belt, unbuckle it to see how easily it releases, then rebuckle it. Don't do these things in a fearful way, thinking, "Oh my god, the place might catch on fire!" or "The car might be in an accident!" Just note these details as you have noted details about various objects of attention. With time, the process becomes as automatic as blinking your eyes when dust blows in your face. Then if you do need to get to the exit in a rush you'll know where it is, or you'll know how to release that seat belt. Fast. Without having to devote conscious thought to locating an exit or releasing a seat belt, you'll be able to focus on other things, such as the shortest distance between you and your child, who you're going to grab and take to safety.

Intuition and analysis are closely related. Even in cases where you have time to process and consider complicated information, odds are that the best response will be the first one that comes to mind—*if* you've taken the time to sit with the question and *if* your information is reasonably good. The more knowledge you have, the better your intuition can operate and the better your analytic ability will be. But life is a series of decisions made with incomplete information. So we do the best we can and heed our intuition.

During the Indian Ocean earthquake and tsunami of 2004, waves up to thirty meters high, about one hundred feet, inundated coastline communities, killing over 230,000 people. In the minutes preceding a tsunami strike, the sea often—not always, but often—recedes temporarily from the coast. On Mai Khao Beach in northern Phuket, Thailand, a ten-year-old British tourist named Tilly Smith had studied tsunamis in geography at school and recognized the warning signs of the receding ocean and frothing bubbles. She and her parents warned others on the beach, which was evacuated safely, saving over one hundred lives. John Chroston, a teacher from Scotland, also recognized the signs at Kamala Bay, north of Phuket, and took a busload of vacationers and locals to safety on higher ground. The actions of Tilly and John were driven by knowledge and a desire to survive and help others to survive.

They reacted quickly as a result of analysis and intuition. They were also centered—as some naturally are—and trusted their own perceptions. If either of them had stopped to second-guess themselves, would they have had time to escape and save others?

Of course both intuition and analysis can be fooled. That could have been a harmless garter snake on the trail. In that instance, jumping first and analyzing later would have done no harm and would have been the best choice. If Tilly Smith had been mistaken, what is the worst thing that could have happened—a little embarrassment?

However, in other ways acting on faulty instinct can lead to tragedy. There have been too many instances to recount of armed people reacting in fear and killing innocents. Guns, like cars, increase our physical power and reach. They do not increase our brainpower. When we drive or use a firearm we are in effect like dinosaurs with tiny brains and large muscles and claws. Therefore we need precise and conscious training and much practice before we drive an auto or use a gun. Having acquired that training, and having done the lessons in this book, we are fully engaged and centered when driving. When driving, we drive. We do not eat hamburgers, talk on a cell phone or do our nails while piloting a couple of tons of steel. Nor do we discharge firearms at shadows because we're frightened of the *possibility* of an assailant being there. Having dealt with our fears and acquired competence with firearms, and being moral persons, we would make certain that there is an actual threat before acting.

Prejudice regarding skin color, gender, sexual orientation, religion or national origin have no place in Taoist thought, or in civilized society. On many occasions such prejudices have led to tragic and fatal incidents. Having worked through the previous lessons on assessing individuals, it would be especially tragic if a reader's assessments were skewed by prejudice regarding superficial characteristics. If there is any possibility that you might have lingering tendencies to judge people by some group they appear to belong to, it might be time for a deeper personal assessment to make sure your mental filters are clear. If you've done the previous training and if your input is clear, you can trust your instincts. But always keep your higher functions engaged. Being centered, aware and directing your attention to matters at hand will not only help you to survive, it will aid you in helping others to survive.

The sage takes care of all men, and abandons no one.

—Lao Tze

ADAPTABILITY

It is not the strongest of the species that survives, nor the most intelligent that survives. It is the one that is the most adaptable to change. —**Darwin**

The ten thousand things carry yin and embrace yang. They achieve harmony by combining these forces. —**Lao Tze**

Adaptability is enjoying the sound of cicadas when the heat is in the hundreds.

Adaptability is soaking the bed clothing in the shower and using it as protection to escape the hotel fire.

Adaptability is enjoying cornmeal when you're ten years old in Sudan and that's all the aid workers have to give you.

Adaptability is making a splint for your broken leg and hobbling five miles to the ranger station and enjoying the fresh, green smell of the forest along the way.

Adaptability is washing your little brother's clothing in the sink so he'll be clean for school.

Adaptability is accepting a person for who they are, not what they are.

Adaptability is making rattraps from discarded tin cans.

Adaptability is figuring out a new recipe to cook those rats.

Adaptability is learning a new language in a foreign country so you can support your family.

Adaptability is pulling together with your neighbors and helping everyone get to safety when your town is flooded.

Adaptability is stripping insulation from copper wires by hand for ten euros a day.

Adaptability is living on five euros a day in Rome and sending five home to Rwanda.

Adaptability is moving your family into a one-room apartment when your house is foreclosed.

Adaptability is deciding to start your own business when your company lets you go after fifteen years and tells you the pension fund is bankrupt.

Adaptability is learning how to live on less and enjoy the art of poverty so you can save to start that business.

Adaptability is being entranced by the antics of a pine marten when it's ten below, snow is thigh deep, your sneakers are soaked and your mom can't buy you boots.

Adaptability is eating those grubs in that log after your food runs out, and you're waiting for the bush plane—and savoring the meal.

Adaptability is making do.

Adaptability is finding a way to carry on and enjoy your life when you lose everything you thought was important.

Adaptability is survival and it costs nothing in money.

INTERPERSONAL INTERACTIONS AND CONFLICT

Sometimes fight, sometimes run, sometimes do nothing.
—Ancient martial arts proverb

For the survivor who has done the preceding lessons, most interpersonal interactions with strangers will be friendly or neutral. However, there may be times when conflict is unavoidable. Conflict takes many forms. Some of the most common forms of conflict in Western culture are the (mostly) male dominance games often engaged in by adolescents, and by adults with adolescent mentalities. Since they often lead to unforeseen consequences—frequently fights—and because they are fundamentally dysfunctional in today's world, dominance games should be avoided by sensible people. Road rage and daily frustrations also often lead to conflict, which in turn can lead to violence. Criminal assault and warfare, which in today's world means the possibility of terrorist attack and kidnapping, are other forms of conflict the survivor should be prepared to handle.

First, let's consider how to deal with the most common forms of conflict. Suppose you've assessed a stranger's attentions and you *see* that he's belligerent and looking for a fight. Perhaps there is a group with him. Your goal is to avoid physical conflict. No matter the provocation, do not engage in fighting of any kind. A fight is when two or more persons agree to exchange violence. Self-defense is one or more persons defending themselves from one or more other person's violence. Self-defense is everyone's moral right.

First option: Pull in your energy bubble. Do not talk, smile or react to verbal provocation. Walk away. Provide him, or them, with no target. Again, and this bears repeating, your object is to avoid or escape physical conflict, not to prove a point, assert your dominance, or demonstrate your lack of intimidation.

Second option: If, for whatever reason, you cannot leave, hold your ground, remain centered and feel your own internal strength. Strengthen your energy bubble, but project no hostility. Be emotionally neutral. Show no fear. If fear has arrived you know what to do with it. In other words, "do nothing" in the Tao sense. Again, your only goal is to avoid or escape physical conflict.

Third option: As in the second option, hold your ground, remain centered, show no fear or hostility and "do nothing" in a more active but not aggressive way. Expand your energy bubble a little so that the other person gets a stronger sense of you. If your assessment and intuition tells you this person would react favorably to a smile and a friendly word, then smile and say something friendly. Often this will defuse the situation, and might even lead to a friendly conversation. If you see no possibility of turning this interaction into a friendly encounter, attempt to distract the other person verbally. Say something totally out of context: "Hey, how about those Lakers," or, "*Avatar,* what a movie." Ask him if he's ever been to Timbuktu. Ask if he believes in aliens. The distraction and resulting conversation—"Yeah, I think aliens are real, too."—might interrupt his script and diffuse the situation.

Fourth option: If he or they move to attack, defend yourself physically without hesitation and do so with full commitment.

If you feel that you cannot defend yourself physically, you need to get some training. We live in a world where the possibility of violence exists. As a survivor, and a person who might have to protect loved ones, you need to be prepared to deal with violence, as you now are with other threats.

Learning self-defense does not require you to become a violent person. You can and should always cultivate a peaceful heart, but learn to defend at need. Teaching physical defense arts is beyond the scope of this book. But based on personal and professional experience, I'll offer some suggestions.

PHYSICAL SELF-DEFENSE

In ancient times in China, Taoist and Buddhist monks developed extremely effective methods of defense, empty-handed and with weapons. Although they carried no weapons, they were proficient in their use. They also learned healing arts and philosophy. These monks traveled constantly, ministering to people, using their healing arts to cure them when sick, advising them on philosophical matters and when necessary aiding them in defense. There were bandits and renegade soldiers wandering the countryside, especially during the Warring States Period. Travel was dangerous and the monks usually traveled alone. To defend themselves, survive and be able to perform their duties to the people, they had to possess extraordinary defensive skills, which they did. They acquired these abilities through years of training in their monasteries. Before they went out to assume their responsibilities in the greater world they had to pass a series of tests to prove their abilities—in healing and philosophy as well as defense. This system worked very well, producing many monks who saved lives with their medical skills and defensive skills, and spread the philosophy of the Tao, or the Tao blended with Buddhism—Chan Buddhism. From this early period, legends grew about the almost mystical abilities of these monks.

However, this system required an apprenticeship of many years, and there was a need for more monks than the system could produce. In response to this need, the monasteries developed systems of defense that could be mastered in months rather than years, and recruited additional young people. This training was always accompanied with grounding in the healing arts, and most importantly a firm foundation in the Tao and/or Chan Buddhism and a commitment to peaceful ways—if possible.

Virtually all of today's Eastern martial arts grew from these systems. Some of these systems ossified over the years, losing touch with their original purposes. Some became sports. Some retained their focus and still today offer effective defensive training. Some also retained the philosophical underpinning of the original teaching, though most lost all of the healing arts component.

As taught by *some* instructors, *some* martial arts can be effective in self-defense—if you invest months and perhaps years in training. If your primary goal is self-defense, seek out training that, after an initial introduction, provides physical contact and simple, easy-to-learn techniques. Spending months learning forms, or *kata,* can be worthwhile and enjoyable for the martial artist, and is very good training, but is beside the point for a person who only wants to quickly learn self-defense.

The grounding you now have in centered movement is fundamental to learning any martial art and to learning to defend yourself. If you decide to train in a martial art, combatives, boxing or wrestling, you will find that being able to move while fully centered will enable you to progress quickly and to move with agility and power.

The shortest route to learning effective physical self-defense is through some form of combatives as used by the U.S. Army Special Operations groups and U.S. Marine Corps, and by other nations' military units, especially the Chinese, Russians and Israelis. Combatives were derived from martial arts and include punching, kicking, grappling and—importantly—weapon disarms. There are competent instructors in combatives in most cities who teach civilian students. Compared to traditional martial arts, combatives can be learned in a relatively short time—at the expense of some bruises, which is part of the learning process. Physical contact teaches you to not be fearful of physical contact, especially if you're centered in Tao space and facing your fears.

If you have no experience of physical violence, and no access to combatives training or good, practical martial arts instruction, start by visiting a boxing gym or a kickboxing gym, or a wrestling or judo training hall. This is, in any event, a good idea in order to see what hard physical contact looks and feels like. However, do not mistake what you see there for self-defense. All of these activities teach useful defensive skills, but self-defense is not the same as a contact sport.

Self-defense is defending yourself and your loved ones by whatever means necessary. Period. Sports such as boxing and wrestling have rules, even if not immediately apparent to the inexperienced eye. Even the popular mixed martial arts matches are sporting contests with rules. Neither opponent is allowed to gouge out eyes, bite, use weapons or bring a few friends to help out. All of these things can and do happen in street fights and criminal assaults. Self-defense has no rules, except to survive—and to not go too far in your own defense. If you have successfully halted the violent attack, do not continue the violence, even if angry. Do only what you must to defend your life, but do all that you must.

If you decide to pursue a particular martial art or defense-related sport such as boxing or wrestling for the enjoyment and mastery of it, do so. But you don't need years of martial arts training or a Golden Gloves boxing trophy to defend yourself.

If you cannot locate a combatives instructor, you may have to go to more than one place to learn what you need. Boxing will quickly teach you how to punch and how to take a hit, valuable skills for self-defense. But the sport of boxing requires top physical conditioning, is divided into weight classes (which real-world violence is not) and has no response to a kicker or wrestler. Kickboxing teaches both punching and kicking, and therefore provides more self-defense skills than Western boxing, but it does not teach grappling, and also requires top physical conditioning to engage in the sport. Wrestling teaches grappling, but does not teach punching, kicking or blocking such blows, and requires top physical conditioning. Like boxing, the sport of wrestling is divided into weight classes and is highly dependent on physical strength and size. A lightweight wrestler or boxer has little chance against a heavyweight opponent in competition, although either could most likely use their skills in effective self-defense in certain situations.

Wrestling, and some forms of judo that are currently popular, concentrate entirely on ground fighting, which can be useful in self-defense. But going to the ground in a real-world attack should be avoided if at all possible. Unlike training halls, streets have curbstones and often broken bottles, things you do not want to fall on. More importantly, going to the ground leaves you open to attack by others. There's an excellent chance that while you're grappling with one assailant, his accomplices will be kicking you or attacking you with clubs and knives. And the ground is the last place you want to be if attacked by a fierce dog.

However, many have trained for short but dedicated periods in each of these sports, long enough to acquire the basics and experience physical contact, and then used that experience coupled with determination and commitment to save themselves from unprovoked attack.

When and if you decide to get some defense training, use your personal assessment skills to evaluate the potential instructors. What kind of energy does he or she project, positive or negative? Are they boastful or modest, confident or arrogant? Is this a person you would trust with your life? That's exactly what you might be doing if you ever have to use what you are setting out to learn. Observe a training class before joining one. What is the nature of the students? Do they look serious? Are they working hard? What is the nature of the interaction between instructors and students, and among students? Are they respectful to each other? Are these people you want to spend time with? Would you trust them to be good training partners?

I have seen good instructors teaching civilians things that have application only for law enforcement or the military. Much of police officer and military training has little application for most people. As a civilian, you do not have arrest powers, or the need to "take out" a sentry. Think carefully and ask yourself if the training seems like something you could use in real life. After meeting an instructor and seeing a class, go home, enter Tao space and focus on the situation and the person. What does your intuition tell you about this prospective trainer and the training? Most importantly, what are you looking for?

Your skills in entering Tao space, centering and moving will greatly aid you in whatever form of defense you decide to pursue—including training with firearms and other weapons. The physical conditioning you've acquired will be of great benefit in training, and in real-life physical conflicts, if any. You might encounter related forms of conditioning in some martial arts and greet it with familiarity. No matter how proficient you become, always cultivate a peaceful heart. Always.

CRIMINALS, CRIME AND EXTREME SITUATIONS

Self or wealth: Which is more precious? —**Tao Te Ching**

The skills you've acquired in awareness will aid you in spotting and avoiding potential criminals. Most of us have an innate sense of a person's intentions. During the previous lessons you've learned to augment and strengthen all your senses, in particular those that help you evaluate people and their intentions. Pay attention to your senses, feelings and intuition. Always be aware of your surroundings and who is in your area. If you feel uncomfortable with a person who's standing or sitting close to you in public, move away from them while retaining awareness of them. If you don't like the vibe of a person who approaches you in public, move away while keeping your eyes on them or maintaining awareness of them and their actions. Do not engage in conversation with them. Awareness and avoidance will eliminate a high percentage of possible criminal attacks.

But what if you're attacked with no provocation or warning? Suppose the person whose vibe made you uneasy attacks without warning, or if the bully who threw that punch at you is a violent psychopath rather than a belligerent bully and he escalates the conflict to deadly violence? Skill in combatives, coupled with the physical conditioning and other skills you've learned in this book, can save your life when confronted with murderous criminal intent if you're ready and fully committed to defending yourself.

Take a few moments, slip into Tao space and ask yourself this: would I fight to the death to save my life or that of a loved one? If the answer is anything other than yes, you might want to do another self-assessment. After doing so, you might want to work on your combative skills. Also, slip into Tao space and ask yourself this question: should you give your money to a robber to avoid violence? If your answer is anything other than yes, you need to do another self-assessment and reflect on the value of money versus life. Once you're clear on these points, you'll probably want to further develop your ability to evaluate another person's intent, even during conflict, so that you can tell the difference between a bully and a psychopathic killer. You'll need to know the difference to act appropriately. As a moral person, you do not want to overreact. Nor do you want to become a victim.

What if you find yourself in the midst of a criminal shooting, such as a robbery or an attack by a mass murderer, or even a terrorist attack? Unless you are a police officer or a soldier, your first objective is to preserve your life and that of your loved ones. Your best chance of doing that may be to duck and cover and escape by crawling or otherwise presenting a low profile, or by disarming the shooter as they reload. But you must evaluate the situation in a split second and act according to the situation. This is where all your previous training in senses, directed attention and centering becomes critical in your decision-making. You should also have a plan. Not detailed plans to cover all eventualities, but some general plans applicable to a variety of possibilities.

HAVING A PLAN, ACCIDENTS AND EXTREME EVENTS

Anticipating situations that might arise and thinking your way through them can help to avoid freezing or flapping during life-threatening incidents. Center, go into Tao space, visualize things that might happen and consider what your best response would be. It might not be comfortable to visualize possible emergency situations, but you must get out of your comfort zone and become comfortable with the unexpected in order to be able to act effectively in a survival situation.

What would you do if your cruise liner ran aground? What if you're exiting the freeway and a car is entering the off-ramp at high speed? What if a neighbor's dog attacks you while you're walking your child in a stroller? What if you find yourself in the middle of a gangbanger shoot-out? What if a police officer mistakes you for a wanted criminal and arrests you at gunpoint? What if there's a mudslide about to engulf your car on your way to work?

It is certainly not pleasant to visualize a person walking into a restaurant, school, movie theater or other public place and randomly shooting people, but these things do happen and you will need to think about a response to this possibility if you want to be prepared to deal with such situations. In America we have a long history of people who seemingly have lost their minds and shoot people in public places. But these incidents are not unique to America. In Norway in 2011 a person shot and killed more than seventy people, more than any mass murderer in America. Similar events occur in other countries where citizens, or subjects, do not possess firearms. We read reports from China about crazed men attacking and killing schoolchildren and people on the street with large kitchen knives. In South Africa, a country with one of the highest murder rates in the world, the weapon of choice is an *assagai*—a spear. Reports come from the Philippines about people "going amok" and killing many people on the street with edged weapons of one kind or another. It appears that there is a tiny number of potential homicidal maniacs in every human population.

The possibility of being raped is repugnant to contemplate. But rape is all too common. I once worked on a pro bono basis with a psychologist at a rape crisis center. I worked with rape victims who had reached the point in their recovery of wanting to learn to defend themselves to further their personal empowerment and to be able to prevent a recurrence of this horrifying event. Every person I worked with, of both genders (yes, men get raped also), said they would fight to the death rather than to again become a rapist's victim. None of them liked to consider this possibility, but all of them did so in order to develop their defenses.

The list of possible dangers is endless and you cannot possibly have a detailed plan worked out for every eventually. However, thinking about various possibilities, without fear and fully centered, can aid your already developed skills: awareness, heightened senses, directed attention and centered physical fitness. If you have worked through all the exercises and lessons in this book and incorporated these practices and skills into your life, you will be far better prepared to deal with any emergency than those who wander through life half-asleep. Adding to these skills by previsualizing possibilities and responses will help to avoid getting caught flat-footed with no idea of how to respond, as will getting additional situation-appropriate training.

When you board a cruise liner you'll note the location of the lifeboats and the shortest distance from your cabin to them, and be aware of their location no matter where you are on the liner. And if the boat appears to be sinking and the public address system is telling you to stay in your cabin and that everything is under control, but you see crew members boarding lifeboats (as happened on an international cruise liner recently), you'll trust the evidence of your own eyes rather than what you're being told. When you drive you are always aware of traffic around you, and of escape routes if a big rig should flip or you encounter that car entering the freeway on the off-ramp. You know that the best thing to do in the event of a random shooting is to duck, cover and exit the area, if possible; in other words, get down and crawl to safety. Do not freeze or flap. If the shooter is within reach and you can't escape, you might decide to disarm and subdue them rather than getting shot while not resisting. If someone goes berserk with an edged weapon, you would do well to run—unless you're on an aircraft and there's no escape, in which case you might have to disarm and subdue the person.

FIREARMS AND OTHER WEAPONS

> *Weapons are instruments of fear; they are not a wise man's tools.*
> *He uses them only when he has no choice.* —**Lao Tze**

The use of any types of weapons is a topic beyond the scope of this book. If you live where armed conflict is prevalent, or where being the victim of violent crime is a high possibility, as a survivor you might do well to arm yourself and learn how to use the arms you select. But unqualified and frightened people have no business with firearms or other deadly weapons. If you decide to learn the use of deadly weapons, do not be satisfied with learning how to operate your weapon at an introductory level. Attain proficiency. Make sure you can employ your weapon quickly and decisively under real-world conditions of darkness, poor footing, confusion and sudden attack. This can only be accomplished by situational training. Be sure your levels of competency, personal fear management and judgment are great enough so that you will not harm innocent people. And always be aware that the law of unintended consequences is magnified when you use weapons.

A good starting place is to read and apply the lessons in my books *The Complete Gun Owner* and *The Tactical Knife*, and then, if at all possible, obtain qualified, competent, hands-on instruction in situational defense. Learning gun handling and shooting on an ordinary shooting range is only a first step in armed self-defense.

We live in a random and sometime violent world. Any of us might be forced to do violence to protect a loved one or ourselves. The only thing worse than being forced to do violence is to witness the death or violation of a loved one, or to have such done to oneself. The decision to arm or not to arm yourself is yours alone. It is not mine. I am neither an advocate nor an opponent of armed self-defense. Arming oneself is a moral issue with legal consequences, an issue that each person must decide for themselves.

Doing lethal violence to another person has nothing in common with ballet-like choreographed movie violence. It is an ugly thing. Use all of your Tao skills to avoid situations wherein you might have to deal with any form of violence, most of all deadly violence. Four hundred years ago John Donne wrote, "No man is an island, entire of itself . . . any man's death diminishes me . . . and therefore never send to know for whom the bell tolls; it tolls for thee."

Like much great literature this contains a simple truth. If you have the great misfortune to be placed in a situation where you must take another's life in order to survive, the experience will change you, and not in any movie macho way. It will diminish you.

SURVIVAL TOOLS AND EQUIPMENT

Amass a store of gold and jade, and no one can protect it.
—Tao Te Ching

The Tao tells us that simplicity and minimalism are best in material things. Practical experience shows this to be true. I have traveled through much of Asia, Latin America, the United States and Europe, camping in wilderness and living in so-called primitive or survival conditions with nothing more than a shoulder bag or small daypack and a few essentials. Taoist and Buddhist teachers and monks I have known do the same, as do many outdoors people and international travelers.

Gear has an insidious way of making us think we are protected simply by possessing it. But being loaded down with equipment will not help us to survive if we lack survival skills. In addition to the skills you have already mastered, learn basics such as firemaking, maintaining your body temperature, how to not get lost and other practical living skills. What we in our urban, technological world consider survival skills, much of the rest of the world considers everyday living skills. So did our recent ancestors. My grandparents knew all of these things; yours probably did also. In other sections, this book provides an introduction to such basic skills and recommends other books to fully develop them.

For the person who knows how to use them, a few tools can save lives. We are, after all, tool users. Just as our prehistoric ancestors did, we come naked into this world. Our remote ancestors survived and built civilizations with simple stone tools. Today experimental archaeologists and expert flint knappers can turn out a stone knife or ax head in a few minutes. You can chop down a tree with a stone ax you can make in less than an hour—if you know how and if you have a supply of the right kind of rocks. But for practical survival you'll probably want more modern tools.

I cannot tell you exactly what tools to carry for your individual circumstances. A uniformed soldier, an international traveler, a nurse who travels only a mile or two to work, a commuter who travels from New Jersey to Manhattan on public transport, a Los Angeles commuter who drives forty miles each day to work—each of these would have different specific needs. However, there are certain basic items that would be useful in urban and wilderness areas and in almost all circumstances.

READY BAGS AND BUG-OUT BAGS

Expanding on the practice of being aware and ready, survivors always carry a few useful tools on their persons, and a few more in a "ready bag," which is a small bag you can carry with you at all times that does not impede your agility or ability to run. Your ready bag can be a laptop or camera bag, a Hermes purse or a scruffy book bag. Any bag that is handy enough to carry daily and is appropriate for your lifestyle will do. If you already carry a day bag, you simply add a few helpful items to it.

I've carried some form of ready bag for most of my life, and will detail a minimal gear list at the end of this chapter. First, to better enable you to determine your own needs let's consider some examples of ready bags.

The first ready bag I ever saw belonged to Wabash Pete, one of my childhood mentors. Wabash Pete lived next to the Wabash River in a small cabin he had built, thus his name. I met him one day when I was fishing. I was ten years old and not catching any fish, until Pete showed me how. Pete was old and whiskered and rumored to be a World War I veteran. He was pretty much a hermit. For some reason he seemed to like me. Over the next year or so he showed me a great deal about how to survive, although he called it "getting by."

Whenever we went "woods wandering," Pete always brought the same beat-up little khaki-colored canvas bag he carried around town. He called it his "possibles bag." In it he had a tobacco tin with fishing gear, his .22 pistol and a little extra ammo, a red bandana, an old kitchen knife in a homemade leather sheath and a tiny sharpening stone, a sandwich in waxed paper and maybe an apple and some peanuts, a surplus army canteen filled with water (which had a special taste—canteen water always does), a half-pint bottle of "snakebite medicine" (I think it was bourbon, but he never let me taste it) and a few other odds and ends like wire for snares. In the pockets of his baggy pants and slouchy jacket he always had cigarettes, a cigarette lighter made from a rifle shell and a waterproof matchbox filled with matches, a pocket compass, some cord and a leather thong, a folding knife, another bandana, a worn leather wallet with a few dollars and sometimes bubblegum or candy for me. If we were staying out overnight he brought a little bag of flour or cornmeal, and rolled up a thin wool blanket inside a rubberized poncho and tied it on the outside of his bag, along with a tin can he used as a cook pot. With these few things, Wabash Pete could "get by" indefinitely. Pete was an expert hunter, trapper and fisherman and knew what plants to eat in season; he was a pretty good camp cook, too. Even without his blanket, poncho and cook pot he could get by fine by building a shelter and fire and cooking in the open fire or on a flat rock.

Note that he carried his possibles bag at all times, and added to it when he planned to be away. This is called a "layered system," the idea being that you always have essential items and add a few comfort items when possible.

In paramilitary training I was instructed in detail how to assemble a bug-out bag (BOB), also known as a ready bag or a go bag . . . or sometimes a "go to hell bag"—referring to when everything goes to hell. This was a small, handy bag that I could easily carry with me at all times, and which contained a *few* essential items of equipment and supplies for use if I had to bug out; that is to say, scram, exit, head for the border, slip out the back, Jack.

The bag was what we called an AWOL bag, basically a gym bag. In it I had a strong sheath knife and a tiny whetstone; a match-grade .22 pistol in a slip holster with three loaded magazines and fifty rounds of ammo; a flyweight, water-resistant, nylon jacket, light wool shirt, hat, thin leather gloves, sunglasses and tightly rolled poncho; a canteen with a cup that could be used as a cook pot; a little food, matches in a waterproof case; a compass and penlight; a scarf to serve as a head net for bugs; a small first-aid pouch; a compact shaving kit; a match case with monofilament, hooks and wire (wrapped with duct tape); twenty feet of parachute cord; a notebook and pen; a pint bottle of "snakebite medicine" (usually Johnny Walker); a paperback book; a good bit of cash and extra identification (kept in the lining of the bag); an extra shirt; and a change of shorts and socks.

This BOB was actually a combination ready bag and travel bag. With this outfit I was equipped for urban and rural travel, work, rough camping, and food foraging and hunting in wilderness areas in Latin America and Southeast Asia. This might sound like a lot of equipment when described in detail, but the weight of the bag and gear was less than ten pounds— lighter than most laptop bags today. The bag was small and unobtrusive and could be placed next to my chair in a restaurant or held on my lap on public transportation without attracting attention. I dressed appropriately for the climate, and also carried a tiny nylon bag with one set of dressier clothing for town. On my person I carried a passport case and passport, cash in three locations, a business card–sized address book with emergency contact information, a folding knife, two handkerchiefs, keys, a Zippo lighter and cigarettes (everyone smoked then). Here's an important point: I used all of these items and replaced them as needed. A ready bag, a ready/travel bag or a BOB must be of everyday utility or soon it will be seen as a burden and left behind, as will "just in case" items.

I soon replaced that gym bag with a camera bag, then various European hunter's pouches and shoulder bags and later a series of small daypacks. The contents of my ready/travel bag has changed somewhat over the years; space blankets, cell phones and lightweight laptops were not available then. Contents also varied, and still do, according to the local environment: sun hat in the tropics, wool cap in winter. I no longer carry a firearm and have limited need for fishing gear in urban areas, but the core items have remained remarkably unchanged over the years.

On one trip I island-hopped for over a month on a local boat through the Sulu Sea with similar gear—substituting the wool shirt and gloves with a sarong, swim trunks and *lots* of suntan lotion. I reached out from the hull of the twenty-foot trimaran and dolphins swam under my hand and let me stroke them. I watched small gales moving across a flat, calm sea. We ate fish caught on a line trailed behind the craft and cooked on an open fire built on a sandbox. When the fish didn't bite we ate rice. When the rice ran out we fasted. We beached our boat on tiny unnamed islands where we traded for papayas and mangos, and the only light came from the sun, moon, stars, and oil lamps in nipa huts. On shore we waited out storms that turned the sky dark and bruised. At all times we lived in what many would consider survival conditions. I thought we were simply living, and my heart was filled with joy.

In Indonesia, I found charcoal tablets for use in case of food poisoning and added them to my first-aid pouch. In various wilderness areas such as the Rocky Mountains and California's Sierra Nevada I have added a lightweight sleeping bag and mat, tarp and additional food, still keeping the overall weight of the ready bag around fifteen pounds. In the Mexican Sierra Madre, where I traveled on foot for weeks at a time and met sorcerers, *drugistas,* and kind, gentle people, I added a wool serape (which served as both warm jacket and sleeping gear), and carried tortillas, jerky

SURVIVAL TOOLS AND EQUIPMENT • **133**

and chilies to supplement locally foraged and purchased food. I never felt underequipped.

WHAT TO CARRY

Judging from what I've read on the Internet, the term *bug-out bag* is now in common usage. But there is little agreement on what constitutes a BOB. Most advocate a large backpack filled with sleeping bag, tent, camp stove, a week's worth of freeze-dried food, a gallon or so of water, fire starters, air filter masks, a water filter, a GPS unit, a CB radio, a satellite or cell phone, laptop or tablet, extra batteries, extra clothing, rain gear, knives, machetes, hatchets, and enough guns and ammunition to arm a fireteam. If you have all this gear, you're camping not surviving—and you'll be camping close to your vehicle because you won't be walking very far burdened with such a load. If you have to run, say from a wildfire or a riot, you'll ditch that big, heavy bag fast. Odds are you won't have that gear with you in the event of an emergency. Most likely it'll be in the trunk of your car or at home.

Less is best. Think about what you need to get by daily and in an emergency. What emergencies are you most likely to encounter? Might you need to walk home during a regionwide power failure, such as those that strike the Northeast from time to time? Do you live in an earthquake zone? Are you traveling to Africa? The unforeseen can occur on vacation as well as at home. Recently, civil disturbances in Bangkok developed into armed conflict. People were killed, buildings were burned and travelers were stuck in their hotels and the airport for days. Such events are not unique. Civil disturbances are common. Your ready bag is the one bag you keep when you must jettison all other luggage and run for the airport, or flee a riot in your own city, or get home after an earthquake or regionwide power outage. If you're ever evacuated by helicopter or plane, your luggage *will* be left behind—but not the small ready bag strapped to your body.

Your ready bag could contain the basics in the list that follows. Add to them situation-specific gear, but not so much you won't want to carry it with you, or that you can't easily carry it while running and jumping. Will you carry your ready bag while walking the streets of Bangkok in hundred-degree weather, to your office or workplace, to lunch or to the store while shopping? Sit with your gear for a while. Slip into Tao space and consider each item. Are you likely to *need* it or do you just *want* it?

Consumerism and marketing drives the demand for specialized survival equipment. There are even trade fairs and shows for the public dedicated to selling survival equipment. Some of these things are functional; most will never be used. You can outfit yourself for outdoor survival in any housewares department, or in a local market or bazaar anywhere. A shower curtain makes a good rain tarp or sunshade. If it's a large size it can be doubled under you and used as a ground cloth. Gauzy curtains serve as effective mosquito netting in many countries, including Italy and Indonesia. The two together fold up to the size of a book, weigh little and cost less than a specialized tent. A fleece blanket, heavy or light according to weather, will keep you as warm as most sleeping bags, except those designed for extreme use. A windshield sunshade makes a functional insulated sleeping pad. A simple book bag will carry this gear, a water bottle and other essentials.

Crowbars and other tools, camping gear, large quantities of food and water are second-line gear, to be stashed at home, in your car or wherever you think you can get to them in an emergency.

In your ready bag or on your person, in addition to a **cell phone, identification,** and other items normally carried, you could carry these items:

- **Extra cash.** Cash is definitely a survival tool. You knew that. It can even be used for tinder to start a fire in the wilderness.
- A **strong, sharp knife,** which is your all-purpose tool.
- A **firesteel,** which is an alloy rod that sparks to make fire.
- A **butane lighter.**
- A **full water bottle** and a **snack**—whatever kind of food you normally eat, and is lightweight and will keep for a day or so. If you have a caffeine habit, carrying a few caffeine tablets in case you can't find a cup of coffee or tea will stave off headaches.
- **Two large handkerchiefs or a scarf** will serve as a dust mask, water filter, hot pad, sunshade or bug net.
- A **tiny flashlight or two with fresh batteries**, for finding your way in total darkness, leading others to safety or signaling.
- A **button compass** to help orient yourself if fogged in or otherwise turned around.
- A **local map.**
- An **emergency whistle,** which can be heard over a much greater distance than your voice.

- A **signal mirror** the size of a business card will throw a reflection for miles.
- **Pen, notebook and a business card–sized address book with emergency information**—electronics can and do fail.
- A minimal **first-aid kit**.
- A **toiletries bag,** including **dental floss,** which is an excellent all-purpose cord and thread.
- A **small repair kit with a little duct tape, needle and thread.**
- **Nylon cord.**
- A **flyweight water-resistant jacket** (in any area other than humid tropical regions). It can prevent hypothermia and will stuff into a sack the size of an orange.
- A **sun or warm hat,** according to the season.
- An **inspirational book** is always welcome, perhaps a pocket edition of the *Tao Te Ching*.
- **Mylar-coated plastic blankets,** usually called "space blankets" or "heat sheets," fold up smaller than a handkerchief, weigh about three ounces, and could save a life. In addition to their primary use they can be used as sunshades or shelters and adapted to many other uses. (I once cut up two of them to make vests for three Boy Scouts I encountered in the Sierra with their scoutmaster, all of whom were hypothermic and suffering from altitude sickness.)

If you're going for a day hike, or otherwise traveling in a wilderness area, add a **small pot or metal cup** in which you can boil water, a **second water bottle** and **water purification tablets.** If in a very wet area add an **ultralight poncho** that compresses into a tiny bag, or one of those inexpensive plastic ponchos you can find almost everywhere. A **firearm** for hunting can be invaluable in the wilderness, if you know how and when to use it.

When detailed, this sounds like a lot of gear. When assembled it will fit into two cargo pockets or a very small bag and weigh much less than most laptops.

Lao Chung Li, a Taoist adept I trained with in Hong Kong, carried a simple canvas shoulder bag every day. In town he carried various potions and herbs for training hall injuries, and certain personal items. When we went to the New Territories overnight or traveled in Southeast Asia he brought the same bag. In it he carried his own special tea and herbs, an enamel cup for brewing his tea and herbs, a toiletries bag, needle and thread, a change of clothes, a six-foot length of thin silk he used as a blanket, a sarong, a sunshade and towel, mosquito coils, matches, two small knives and a bottle of "yellow wine." I carried my usual ready bag. We slept in village homes and under trees, bought food in local markets and from villagers, foraged wild vegetables and caught fish. We saw cliffs of cascading orchids, a troop of mischievous monkeys, elephants, clear running streams and sunrise filtered through jungle treetops. Always we traveled easily, walking lightly, going with the Tao.

TWO BASIC LIFE AND WILDERNESS SKILLS

I think of the ability to make fire and to not get lost as life skills rather than wilderness skills. Many people get lost in strange cities as well as in the wilderness, and in much of the world firemaking is an everyday need. Many urbanites who backpack or otherwise venture into wilderness areas lack these two simple and easy-to-learn skills. This lack keeps the search-and-rescue people busy, and has led to many tragedies.

Be well grounded in all outdoor skills before entering a wilderness area. Many backpackers live in a bubble of equipment, walk only on well-marked trails and haven't the least idea of how to avoid getting lost or how to survive without their gear. This is not the way, the Tao.

As you enter any wilderness area, do what you know how to do: slip into Tao space, extend all of your senses and perception and tune in to the local environment, as in previous lessons. Dress appropriately for the climate and terrain. Have extra garments and a sleeping bag or other insulation sufficient to spend the night out, even if you're not planning to do so. Have your ready bag.

You really shouldn't set foot on a wilderness trail—in the United States or in other countries—unless you can build a fire under local conditions and can avoid getting lost. These are minimal skills for the survivor, but critical ones. For detailed instruction in wilderness survival see the books I recommend in the "Suggested Reading" section. Below are basic instructions in how to not get lost and firemaking.

STAYING FOUND

When my sons were about five years old I taught each of them an effective method to avoid getting lost, one used by native hunters I have traveled with in Latin America and Asia to find their way home through thick jungle and trackless rainforests, a method that on some level you probably already use.

The method is simple in the extreme: pay attention to the ground you cover. As you travel, look behind you to see what the land, or city streets, will look like on your return. Take note of landmarks. When you want to return, retrace your steps.

If you're centered and aware, when you look behind you will note in detail what you see: turnings of the trail, the width and curves of the stream, an ancient tree now fallen, the gravel in the dry wash, the scent of the swamp water and those red flowers. These details are all waymarks that will lead back to your starting place. You'll note how the land rises or falls underfoot, and keep track of how many left and right turns you made on the forest roads.

If you're in thick and unfamiliar jungle or forest and you doubt your ability to remember your way—all that underbrush looks the same to you—make your own waymarks. Break branches or small saplings so they hang over your back trail, or scratch a waymark on a boulder, or cut a small mark on the side of a tree. A little cut won't hurt the tree. If you're in the desert and you don't trust your memory, make small stacks of stones or line up rocks forming arrows as you go.

We've all read the story of Hansel and Gretel, who left a trail of pebbles through the forest and used them to find their way home. When they used breadcrumbs for the same purpose, the birds ate them, leaving them lost in deep forest where they encountered the wicked witch. If you're way-marking, make sure you can see the marks from the direction from which you'll be returning, and that the birds won't want to eat them.

If a sudden fog comes down and obscures all waymarks, stop and wait for it to clear. A compass (and knowledge of how to use it) would be helpful in this situation, as it is in most places, as is a map and the ability to read it. (Refer to the "Suggested Reading" section for books on how to use a compass and read a map.) But before you learn how to use a compass—no, the needle doesn't point to where you want to go; it points to north—and before you learn to read a map, remember to look where you've been.

The Australian aborigines use a similar method to find their way across hundreds of miles of wilderness. As they go, they "sing the land." Song-lines mark routes across the land. These paths are passed on in songs and stories, which describe the nature of the land, landmarks and water holes. When traveling on foot through unfamiliar territory, a person can make up their own songline as they go. Rhyming and poetry, like songlines, were used by preliterate people to memorize vast amounts of information. We literate folks may not have such well-developed memories. In that case, making notes or drawing a simple route map in your pocket notebook as you go will work quite well to keep you from getting lost.

Some years ago my wife and I and two of our young sons spent the summer jumping on and off trains from one end of Europe to the other. At the start of the journey, as we left each station I stopped the boys and told them to turn around and look at the station—the name of the station was usually on a sign—and then turn around and look again when we were some way from the station, and to repeat this every block or so, and at every turning until we reached our hotel or pension. In this way they could see where they had been and be able to find their way back. If separated we would meet at the information desk in the train station. After we settled in at a hotel or pension and were going out, I instructed them in the same way, having them stop and look at the front of the hotel, and as we went along to note street names and landmarks. I also made sure each of them had in a pocket a business card of the hotel or pension with address or phone number. After the first weeks I told each of them to start doing this on their own without my direction.

In a small town in Denmark, our youngest, who was seven, had so blithely ignored my instructions to look behind I was sure he wouldn't be able to find his way if lost. He was so happy and in the moment I was reluctant to intrude, but parental duties overrule all. I stopped him at the end of the train station platform and said, "I bet you don't have any idea where you are."

He thought for a moment and confidently replied, "Oh yes I do."

"Tell me, then," I said.

He beamed, triumphantly replying, "I'm with you."

Of course we all laughed. He was perfectly right. And his response was perfectly Taoist in nature, although he had never heard of the Tao. He simply lived it, as do most children until they grow out of it. We continued to work on the exercise because, although his answer was correct, he still needed to learn how to not get lost. As with all other skills in this book, being centered, using directed attention and awareness brings success.

FIREMAKING

Fire can save you when you're stuck in the wilderness. It can keep you from dying of hypothermia, cook food, scare off predators, signal rescuers and provide much-needed cheer when spirits flag. Firemaking seems to be a great mystery to many. It need not be. To build a fire you only need an **igniter, tinder, kindling, fuel** and **oxygen**—and the knowledge of how to use these things.

An **igniter** can be a match, a lighter, a firesteel or sparker, flint and steel, a flare, an electric spark or a magnifying glass, if there's sunlight. You can also use friction—if you know how to generate enough heat by friction to get a coal, which is an advanced skill not detailed in this book. For our purposes, we'll stay with matches, lighters and firesteels or sparkers. You can learn about more esoteric igniters and their use in other books found in the "Suggested Reading" section. Igniters are tiny, weigh next to nothing and could save your life. It's very difficult to find a replacement for them in the wilderness. They're also convenient to light your barbeque.

Firesteels, or sparkers, are excellent igniters. While they do not throw a spark the size of a solar flare, they do throw a hot spark that will catch any good tinder. Firesteels come with instruction on how to use them. They are not subject to being rendered useless by water, as are matches, and are not affected by cold, as are butane lighters. Even the smallest-size firesteel, which can fit on your key ring, will last for thousands of uses.

Butane lighters provide a flame, rather than a spark, are excellent igniters and last for thousands of uses, too. Most will find them easier to use than a firesteel. The best-quality lighters are reliable, although sub-ject to be being affected by cold. If they get too cold they will not ignite. Even in the coldest weather you can avoid this by carrying them inside your clothing.

Even though they produce a flame, I consider matches to be the third choice as igniters. Their flame lasts only for a short time and even the "waterproof" matches can fail if immersed in water. However, they are effective igniters and available almost anywhere.

Prepared survivors always have three igniters available. It's a simple matter, and cheap insurance, to have a pack of matches and a butane lighter in your pocket or ready bag and a firesteel on your key ring.

Tinder is anything that will easily catch fire and burn long enough and hot enough to start kindling burning. Paper, cloth, weeds, dry leaves, wood shavings, pine resin, Spanish moss, tree fungus, bark, rotten wood, wood dust, fibers from a carpet, lint from a dryer, a scrap of cloth from your clothing—all can be used as tinder. Good tinder catches fire easily and must be *dry*.

Kindling is small pieces of wood or other flammable material—anything that burns hot and long enough to start fuel burning. When collecting wood kindling for a fire, you should gather it in graduated sizes, from toothpick-sized to pencil-sized to finger-sized and wrist-sized. Other kindling, such as auto seat covers and seat belts, small rubber tubes, hose strapping and belts, and carpet and upholstery strips, should be torn into graduated sizes before use. Kindling also needs to be *dry*.

Fuel is anything that will burn, most commonly wood. If wood is being used as fuel it should, like kindling, be gathered and cut or split into graduated sizes, starting with wrist-sized and going to larger-sized if you want or need a large fire. Many of the things you can use as kindling can also be used for fuel in larger sizes. It's best if fuel is dry, but if you have enough kindling you can sometimes use damp fuel.

Oxygen is present all around us, but its lack is a common cause of failure in firemaking. Piling too much kindling and fuel on tinder will smother the spark and initial flame.

Firemaking is not difficult if you direct your attention to the details. As in many things, the devil is in the details. Select a spot for your fire that is clear of debris so that your fire will not get out of control and spread. Before igniting a fire, gather all the materials so that you can add them as you progress. Ignite the tinder and place it under the smallest kindling, which you can arrange as a tepee, log cabin or other structure that allows air to flow freely around the kindling. When the smallest kindling catches, gradually add larger kindling until you have a good flame. Then, careful not to smother your fire, add fuel starting with the smallest size and gradually increase until you have the size fire you need.

In Greek legend, Prometheus brought fire to man and Zeus punished him for giving a gift that gave man godlike power. In Chinese legend, Fu Xi, the first ruler of the world, gave fire to man; he was not punished. That Prometheus was punished and Fu Xi was not probably says something profound about the contrast between East and West, but I'm not sure what, so I'll leave it to you to figure out. Every culture has myths about fire, probably because it is the ability to make fire more than any other thing that enabled the start of civilization. Fire is as important now as at the awakening of *Homo sapiens*. Without fire, cars and many other things would not work—and you could freeze to death.

LIFE, SURVIVAL AND THE TAO

GOING WITH THE FLOW, OR AGAINST IT

Do you ever feel like you're surfing life's wave, that everything is cool and you're in the right place and doing the right thing? If you do, that's the Tao and you're living and flowing with it. Feel its currents and eddies and gently guide your life to stay in its flow.

Have you ever felt like you've hit a wall so hard you feel like a bug hitting a windshield at sixty miles an hour, that everything you do goes wrong and nothing is right and every time you pick yourself up you get knocked down again? You're fighting upstream against the Tao. Time to go into Tao space and focus on feeling your life. What parts feel right and good? What parts feel wrong? When you think about the totality of your life, what parts do you shy away from thinking about? It might be time to change course and find that place where you feel like you're just easing along, flowing with life's currents.

Have you ever been in a crowd when suddenly there's a loud noise and the crowd starts running towards the noise and you can't see what's ahead, and it could be Fourth of July fireworks, or a shooting, and you decide to step sideways and let the crowd go? You moved with the Tao. Going with the flow, the Tao, doesn't mean running with the herd towards what might be a cliff.

If you've made the skills in this book part of your life, you will become tuned in to the Tao and sense the flow of your life and of immediate events. You'll come to recognize patterns in events and life, and know whether the events that are developing will lead where you want to go. You'll sense trouble before it's in your face, recognize it when it arrives and work on the problem until it's resolved.

ASKING FOR HELP—FROM GOD, THE UNIVERSE, YOUR GUARDIAN ANGEL, WHATEVER

When survivors have been asked how they survived an "unsurvivable" disaster, virtually every one of them says they asked for help from some unseen force. Taoists believe there is a force that permeates the universe, gives life to all things, is invisible, unfathomable, ineffable and always present everywhere, and that it can be called upon to provide help. Whether you believe in a particular god, many gods, or no god at all; whether you believe in a universal force that can and might assist you— ask for help. Just throw the request out and into the void. It can't hurt and you might be surprised.

GIVING UP

I sometimes read about people giving up in survival situations. What does it mean to give up in a survival situation? What do you give up? Life? How do you give up life? Why give up life? No matter how difficult, painful and horrible life might become, no matter how much you're suffering, life is still to be lived. Aron Ralston is widely known for surviving a wilderness accident during which he amputated his own arm to save his life. Terrible conditions can be overcome. You can strive to live for a better day. Or if to die, then to die trying to live. Giving up has no place in life.

DEATH

Thus shall ye think of this fleeting world:
A star at dawn, a bubble in a stream;
A flash of lightning in a summer cloud;
A flickering lamp, a phantom, and a dream.
—Diamond Sutra

In classic Taoist training, facing death comes first. I've left it till last because we in the West do not deal well with death, and because in Western thought death is the end. In Eastern thought death, like birth, is a beginning.

An exercise that young monks do as part of their basic training is to spend the night alone in a place where dead bodies are held awaiting cremation. There they meditate on the bodies and come to understand that this is the fate of all the billions of people now alive, all the billions who lived before and everyone they know and love. In their deepest hearts they come to realize and accept that they too will surely one day be as these around them are now. They go through all the emotional stages that a terminal patient goes through: fear, denial, anger, depression and, finally, acceptance. In this acceptance they find freedom. In the morning, almost without exception, they emerge lighthearted, free and laughing. They have come to understand, truly understand deep in their hearts, that death is the inevitable result of living. With acceptance comes freedom from that primordial fear, a great joy in life and a commitment to live life to the fullest.

The monk's experiences are similar to those of many who have near-death experiences, and emerge with a renewed purpose and love of life and find each day precious. It is not necessary to spend the night with lifeless bodies to vanquish the fear of death, although it is liberating. You can achieve a level of freedom from fear of death by using the methods you are now familiar with. In the previous example of the young man who was terrified of flying, we saw that under his fear of flying was a deeply rooted fear of death. Once that fear was vanquished he walked forward into the rest of his life free and joyful, head up, fully engaged in life and ready for whatever came next.

You are going to die. You know that intellectually. But have you accepted death in your heart? Are you ready to die? There's an eternity of difference between accepting the inevitability of death and being ready to die, and giving up on life or wanting to die. Love life and you will fight to keep it as long as you can. Be ready to die and you'll live with joy and be truly free.

Fear of death is deeply rooted in our psyches and souls. It is often hidden under other fears, and often dealt with by busyness, distraction and denial. Fear of death leads many people to fill up their lives with things that seem important and must be done. Day after day they fritter away the precious gift of life, until they must die and discover they forgot to live. Fear drives people to work their lives away at jobs they hate. Fear keeps people from pursuing their dreams. Some are comforted by belief in an afterlife. Whether we believe in an afterlife or not, many of us lead our lives running scared. When we awaken at 3:00 in the morning with our hearts pounding, we know this to be true.

Living in abject fear and denial of the inevitable can lead to drug addiction and alcoholism, as if blotting out consciousness slows death's approach; to religious fanaticism, as if clutching to a belief provided a life raft on death's seas; to the obsessive pursuit of wealth and its manifestations, as if the laying up of goods could forestall the arrival of that which awaits us all. Fear of death prevents people from seeing others as they truly are, from experiencing the astounding, magical, wonderful, horrible, glorious world we live in.

Fear of death leads people to make foolish decisions and to constrict their lives in an attempt to be safe, safer and safest. Fear of death manifests as obsessive concern about security, excessive preparation for any possible disaster, overreaction to any perceived threat. Fear of death drives people to carry guns in pleasant suburbs that haven't had a violent crime since Nixon was president. Much of the current wave of survivalism is nonrational and fear driven. If you face death, accept its inevitability and become ready to die; you will vanquish fear and open the door to a free and fearless life.

If you've worked your way through some of your fears by utilizing the methods in the previous lesson on fear, you might be ready to take on the most profound fear, the one at the center of our lives. If you are ready, pick that which you fear most and make it the object of your lesson. Do what you now know how to do. Slip into Tao space and visualize your worst fear that leads to death. See it in all its terrible detail. Feel it. Experience it and follow it all the way to and through death's door. What lies on the other side remains a mystery.

What the caterpillar calls the end, the rest of the world calls a butterfly. —**Lao Tze**

AFTERWORD
LIVING IN THE TWENTY-FIRST CENTURY
Visions of Apocalypse, a Return
to Eden, a Time of Possibilities

The Tao that can be told is not the eternal Tao. —**Lao Tze**

The quotation above is the first statement of the *Tao Te Ching*. Simply put, it means that the flow of the universe, the Tao, cannot be encompassed or defined by a name; that to understand the Tao you must experience it.

To truly experience the Tao we would need to go beyond the practicalities in this book and into a form of directed attention, or meditation, focused on perceiving all things as they are. This can be the pursuit of a lifetime, or it might come in a moment. I hope that through the practical processes in this book, in addition to useful skills, the reader gained a glimpse through "the gate to all mystery" that Lao Tze wrote about in the *Tao Te Ching*—the shadow that lies behind this world we see with our eyes—and saw deep into their own hearts. In those experiences lies an understanding of the universe and our relationship to it deeper than words can describe. From that comprehension flows true survival behavior: compassion for our fellow humans and all living creatures, respect for the natural world and humility before the ineffable.

In its external manifestations, the world we live in has changed almost beyond recognition since Lao Tze wrote the *Tao Te Ching* twenty-six hundred years ago. During the few years since this new century began, the rate of change has sped up so much that it feels like someone has their finger on a global fast-forward button and is holding it down. Remember in the classic movie *The Wizard of Oz* when Dorothy first sees the land of Oz, where her house has landed after being carried away by a tornado? She looks around at the strange and beautiful place and says to her dog, "Toto, I've a feeling we're not in Kansas anymore." The change that Dorothy experienced pales in comparison to the change we're all experiencing—if we're awake and paying attention.

We're not in Kansas anymore, or the twentieth century. We're living in a world so different than that of the past century that many of us suffer from "future shock." Unlike Oz, the twenty-first century is not located "over the rainbow." It's right here, right now and there is no yellow brick road leading to an emerald city where a mighty wizard will solve our problems. After taking the journey with Dorothy and her companions, we learned that the wizard's only power was in bringing out the inner strengths of Dorothy and each of her companions. This is all any wizard can do, in Oz or in our world.

If we look at the dark side our future looks bleak. Many of us prefer to not see the dark side, to live in denial. But doing so will not help to improve our lives or those of our children. We must first see what needs to be changed in order to make changes. And we must understand that we have the power to make those changes. The ancient yin and yang symbol of the Tao shows both darkness and light because that is the nature of the universe, and to remind us that only by dealing with darkness can we find our way to the light.

Looking at the dark side, we see that we're constantly at war. We make war against murderers and criminals who style themselves as freedom fighters and whom we call terrorists. We make war against drugs and imprison thousands of hapless drug users, no more addicted and no more dangerous to themselves or anyone else than the millions who need baskets of pharmaceutical drugs or a fifth of whisky each day to deal with their lives. We make war against cancer and other diseases, rather than simply trying to find cures. The metaphor of war runs through all our society and has become embedded in our psyche, making it the default solution to our problems. We mobilized great armies to fight a resource war that has continued for almost a decade. Drums are now beating to start the second resource war of the century, with more to come if we continue on this path. Politics has devolved into a mean-spirited war of words. Civilized discourse is noticeable by its absence.

The global economic and financial system lurches and staggers from crisis to crisis, narrowly avoiding disaster like a drunken sailor stumbling along a sidewalk clutching at lampposts to avoid falling in the gutter. We worry what will happen if this fragile system collapses, destroyed by its own high priests who, worshiping the god of greed, betrayed our trust and committed the largest theft in history. We wonder why those who engineered this theft are not punished.

Most lesser-developed nations, sometimes grouped together as the Third World, are ruled by an oligarchy, a tiny ruling class that owns virtually everything. These are countries where there is no middle class; where only the poor pay taxes and those taxes go into the pockets of the wealthy; where potholed roads and collapsing bridges are normal and little or no money is spent to improve them; where public schools are underfunded, teachers are overworked and the best chance for a good education is in expensive private schools; where military, police and security organizations are feared by a cowed and propagandized populace; where tent cities and slums proliferate and the homeless live on the streets; where there is no health care except for the wealthy. Sound familiar? It should. America is rapidly becoming a Third World country. By some measurements, such as income inequality, it already is.

Every time I now go to a foreign consulate in the United States, I meet other Americans who are there not to get a travel visa, but to emigrate, to leave America in search of a better life. Formerly employed craftspeople, teachers, office workers and ordinary people now ply their trades, or learn new ones, or teach English in Thailand, China, Turkey, Moldova, Ukraine, Germany, France and dozens of other countries. Never before in decades of travel have I witnessed people *leaving* America to seek opportunity.

Our food supply has been corrupted in the pursuit of profit. Mad prophets spout "end of time" fantasies, and their followers are mesmerized by visions of apocalypse. Pusillanimous politicians perform on the popular media, attacking each other in public and making deals with the same big money interests in private. The airwaves and the Internet are choked with hate-spewing troglodytes. Things have gotten weird and they're getting weirder.

All of this has happened before. Over thousands of years, during all of history, we have seen the rise and fall of civilizations and of their ruling classes.

When the court is arrayed in splendor, the fields are full of weeds, and the granaries are bare. —**Lao Tze**

What differs today from the past is the global reach of the signs and portents that point towards the fall of the kingdom. You might live in one of the few remaining nice suburbs where life continues in a clean, untroubled, hermetic bubble. But no bubble, no matter how strong, no matter how much money has been spent to create it, can protect its inhabitants from the world we have created. We live in a new age that scientists have named the Anthropocene. The previous age, the Holocene, a geological epoch that began at the end of the Pleistocene around twelve thousand years ago, is over. This new age, the Anthropocene, is characterized by human impact on, and alteration of, our environment. We've fouled our nest with industrial and automotive pollution, cut down forests older than our species and drained aquifers of pure water that will take ten thousand years to replace. Our monoculture agricultural practices deplete the soil. The human population of the planet now exceeds seven billion and continues to grow. We've overpopulated the planet and used up resources that cannot be replaced in our lifetimes or our children's children's children's lifetimes.

Multinational corporations have acquired power and influence equivalent to kingdoms of old. Many of those corporations have corrupted national governments, subverted regulatory agencies and deceived the public about the nature of their products with disinformation more sophisticated than any propaganda produced by governments. Some of those products are deadly to all life. Technology that once seemed to offer benefits for all of mankind has now turned on us. Like captive dragons, nuclear plants breathe deadly radiation that spreads over the entire world. The cars that gave us so much freedom, to drive Route 66 or just to better jobs, now choke us with their disease-laden fumes.

In our globalized world, the butterfly effect—when a small change in one location affects the entire system—is a reality. A chicken catches the flu in Hong Kong, passes the disease to people and they die, and air travel around the world comes to a halt. A country becomes a failed state and many of its inhabitants flee to another country, precipitating a crisis in their new country. A small change in banking regulations in the United States creates a loophole for criminals, and the economy of the entire world is affected. A chemical company sells its pesticides to farmers in Indiana and within a few years this deadly poison is in use around the world, stimulating evolutionary adaptation of the targeted pests and creating new resistant forms of pests.

In our bones we sense that our species is headed for the edge of a cliff if we do not change course. Unconsciously or consciously, whether in denial or acceptance, we sense catastrophe looming in our near future. The worldwide popularity of the epic science fiction movie *Avatar*, and to a lesser degree the popularity of television wilderness survival shows, is due to a form of escapism and driven by a profound desire to return to a simpler time, or go to a greener world—to Eden. The center is not holding. Does that rough beast now slouch towards Bethlehem?

Excepting the global nature of the new century, our situation has similarities with the Warring States Period in ancient China, when kingdoms fell and people were forced to flee their enemies with little more than what they could carry—when they were ready at all times to leave through the eastern gate. But our enemies seem to be ourselves. From whom do we flee? Where is our eastern gate? To where will the survivalists with their bug-out bags bug out?

As the Tao shows us, darkness is balanced by light—eventually. This is also a time of great possibility. If you have learned anything from this book, I hope you will have learned to hold to your true center, see the world as it is in all its ugliness and splendor, and to be fearless. We live in dark days, and returning to the light will require fearless people and much work. The butterfly effect, combined with our connectedness, allows the rapid spread of information, informing millions of people of these new threats and enabling us to counter them. Little by little, informed people are beginning to assume powers formerly left in the hands of governments and assuming personal responsibility for making a better world. Therein lies the yang to the yin of possible apocalypse.

In addition to being inhabited by trolls and troglodytes, the Internet is also bringing people from around the world into closer contact and fostering greater understanding. Many of us are reaching out to others without waiting for the creaking machinery of government. We are forming organizations to improve the quality of life for all of us, to save and nurture the planet's resources, to support artists, writers and entrepreneurs, to educate disadvantaged people in many countries. New sources of energy are being developed, and we are waking up to climate change and the reality that we either educate people to control old tech industrial expansion and population growth or we will overrun the world's resources and create a dystopian future where each will be against all. Investigative journalists, independent scientists, individuals and groups work to counter the influence of corrupt corporations and governments by informing the public, raising awareness and creating movements in opposition. Others are building new kinds of organizations to solve problems that our governments have proven to be inept at solving. We now see that politicians are like band majors who wait to see where the people are going then run to catch up and get in front of the parade, and that there's little use in waiting for a politician to make things better. The wizards of our world have no more power than the Wizard of Oz, and we know now that wizards can do nothing more than show us our own power. It's up to us to change what needs to be changed.

> *In the universe great acts are made up of small deeds.*
> **—Tao Te Ching**

Bunkering up and waiting for the apocalypse, or dancing on the edge of the cliff waiting for the tsunami, is not survival behavior. Our society appears to be in the midst of a slow-motion train wreck, and our best hope of survival is to reach out to others, engage for the greater good and act beyond narrow self-interest. But how do we help others if we cannot help ourselves? How can we effect change if we have to work and pay bills to live? It's easier than you might think.

All of us can make small changes in our schedules to allow time to become involved with others and work together for the mutual welfare of all. All too many of us are busy, busy, busy; wrapped up in activities that seem important at the time, and activities that distract us from the drudge of work we dislike. If you do feel trapped in your daily life and would like to have more freedom, you can make that happen using the skills you have learned in this book, and by a few simple, but perhaps not easy, changes in your life.

First, go into Tao space and visualize your life. *See* your days as they pass, *see* your relations with your family, your coworkers and your employer if you have one. Are you happy with your life, or would you like to change it? If you would like to change your life, visualize your life as you would like it to be. *See* the changes you would have to make to create your new life. Change of any kind can be frightening. But you now know how to deal with your fears by facing them. Go into your fears one by one. Are you afraid to quit doing work you dislike? How will you and your family live? Answer those questions by visualizing each step of the process: quitting your job or closing or selling your business, perhaps moving to another neighborhood or town or even country, adjusting to life with less income, perhaps living on savings while starting your new life. As with other fears, these kinds of fears vanish when faced. As with other fears, you must also deal with them in the physical world.

Whether you work freelance or you're the king's man, getting off the consumer treadmill of work and spend, work and spend, will lead you to personal freedom and provide the time needed to do more than work and buy and pay and pay and pay. Distinguish between needs and desires by going into Tao space and considering each thing that costs money. Spend only for what you need. We spend time to get money and that money becomes, literally, our time—the very substance of our lives. Each dollar represents a period of time traded from our lives to obtain it. Ask yourself if you really want to trade a part of your life for the latest gizmo or fashion, if that which you're spending money for is something you'll be glad you bought in twenty years, or near the end of your life when you're counting days. Put away every penny you do not need, but don't forget that we need to have some fun along the way. Misery is no part of the Tao, and having pleasure in your life costs little or nothing. There is no amusement park that provides as much pleasure as simply *seeing* and being absorbed in our world. There is no television show on an expensive wide-screen, or movie that costs a day's wages, that provides more and deeper pleasure than walks with your family, games you play together, reading and talking over meals.

Make it a goal to save a year's income. In that direction lies survival and freedom, the freedom to choose, to buy that small plot of land in the country, to start your own business, to live your dream of becoming an artist, or traveling the world, or simply to not have to work your life away to pay for things you don't need. Once that freedom is gained you can easily devote some of your time to working towards creating a better world. If you do not feel trapped, if you have an excess of money and are comfortable in your life, it's even easier to devote some time and resources to the general welfare. Perhaps you already do so. If so, please continue.

Although gold dust is precious, when it gets in your eyes, it obstructs your vision. **—Hsi-Tang**

Two oceans and a media bubble have created an America that is a hermetic, self-referential society; one in which media can demonize the people of another country—if we've never been to those countries and met those people. Experience the planet we all live on and its fabulous cultures; meet its people and you'll not be taken in by a politician's propaganda and self-serving but hidden motives.

International travel is now within the reach of almost all who are motivated to travel and who make it a priority. Yes, some places are dangerous, as are some people. Don't go to war zones. The rest of the world isn't all that dangerous. Go with an open mind and all skills fully engaged. Be centered, relaxed and open to differences. Smile. Enjoy the ride, the places, the people. The vast majority of people are friendly, or at least not unfriendly or hostile. The world is mostly made up of decent people living their lives. Just like in your hometown.

> *He who knows how to live can walk abroad*
> *Without fear of rhinoceros or tiger.* —**Tao Te Ching**

If you get off the consumer treadmill, define your basic needs and save, you can see—really *see*—the world and meet its people. Take the kids. Not for a two-week vacation. Take an extended journey wherein other places become part of your life; it will change your life, and for the better. Anyone can do it and many do. If you'd like detailed information about how to travel with the Tao, see my soon-to-be-published *The Tao of Travel,* a book that can enhance your experience of travel.

> *A good traveler has no fixed plans and is not intent upon*
> *arriving.* —**Lao Tze**

When you return home, stay in touch with the friends you made. Invite them to come visit and meet your family and friends. Understanding and compassion for others is sound survival practice.

I have lived in countries whose people experienced economic and governmental collapse, war on their own soil, anarchy and famine. Ordinary people do not survive in these beleaguered countries by bunkering up, arming themselves and fearing their neighbors. They survive by cooperation and interdependence, by forming communities and villages—even within megacities such as Mumbai, India. From tribe to country, the history of humanity is not only of conflict, but of mutual dependency.

As I write this, I'm living in a village not far from a location that archaeologists and historians tell us might be the location of the mythical biblical Eden. It is a sprawling area that twelve thousand years ago was lush and green with every kind of fruit and vegetable growing wild, and thickly inhabited by wildlife. It would have been paradise for a society based on hunting and gathering.

But agriculture changed the nature of human society and altered the planet. Where Eden might have once been is now a barren desert. We can dream about Eden, but it's too late to return. There are too many of us. We must survive in the world we have created. And we can survive and live well, if we can but find our way. Humans muddle along. We make do. We can survive if we again learn what we all once knew.

The village I now live in is little different than villages in this part of the world have been for a thousand years. Here men build with stone. All around us are stone walls, steps, plazas, verandas and houses. Over the past weeks I've watched two men building a stone wall on the road leading up the hill to our house. They patiently chip away at large blocks, rounding or flattening them to fit into the space between the last stone they laid and the next one they will place. They wear slouch caps and worn clothing and have hands as rough as the stone they work. A short walk from our house are stone ruins of cities built by Romans, and before them Greeks, before them Lycians, and before them others, going back to long, long before the beginning of what we call civilization. To the east, men built gigantic stone monuments twelve thousand years ago, the oldest man-made structures yet discovered. Little is known of those people, except that they hunted and gathered, built and lived.

Here in this tiny village on the side of a steep hill next to the sea, we found a way of life that has almost disappeared from western Europe, and one that has entirely disappeared from America. In our village, each house has a small plot of land on which people plant and grow grapes and olives, lemons, oranges, figs, eggplant, tomatoes, arugula, cabbage, three kinds of peppers, and onions. Almond, walnut and cherry trees line the village lanes. In the summer's last heat the villagers make wine from their grapes, and dry cherries and figs on clean white cloths under the midday sun. Cherries that are not eaten in season or dried are preserved in jars and stored in the cool room, along with olives in large ceramic jars, baskets of almonds and walnuts, and tubs of goat cheese. Peppers are dried and ground to make paprika, or put up in jars with olive oil. Everyone has chickens, which cluck about, pecking at insects. Goats are tied out on long ropes to crop weeds and gathered into pens come evening. Some houses have a cow or two. There's a carpentry shop, a small general store, a school. Traveling traders drive their vans along the graveled streets cut into the hillside and honk to announce their arrival. Dogs wander freely, as do cats.

Our neighbors knock on our door and bring us produce from their gardens: olives they've cured in tall jars, fresh eggs, rolled and stuffed grape leaves from their kitchen, home-baked cakes and cookies. My wife cooks and sends out dishes of her own creation in return. A man at the end of the road has a chain saw. He delivers sawn logs to our next-door neighbor, who splits them with his ax and gives back some of the split wood in payment. Matrons in brightly flowered baggy pants and headscarves carry two-liter jugs of goat's milk to their neighbor's houses and return home with freshly baked bread.

This is not an isolated paradise. People here have cars, cell phones and high-speed Internet connections. They are connected to the wider world, educated and well informed regarding international events and global conditions. Education here is free, and universal health care affordable and available for all. Families rarely have more than two children and no one goes hungry.

Some villagers nurture and cull the tourist herd during its annual migration each summer to a nearby tourist town, a charming place structured like a sheep-shearing operation where people from dozens of countries come to enjoy the clear seas and green hills. The main street is a long stock chute, much like any livestock chute designed to channel the sheep, cows or goats to the waiting farmer. The main street runs downhill, lined on each side with pensions, shops and cafés. The tourist herd enters at the top of the hill and makes its way down towards the harbor. The slow, the hesitant, the outliers are the first to be snagged by charming merchants as they pass various enticements, but eventually all succumb and are sheared clean as any spring lamb.

Feeding, watering and amusing a few thousand head of tourists each summer provides cash for cars, computers, cell phones, for new stoves and additions to houses, and to send children to be educated in faraway universities. But local primary schools are good, teachers are respected and roots in the village remain strong. Few here bend the knee to corporate masters. The local enterprises are in fact local, and the way of the grape and olive endures. If the tourists disappeared, life here would continue much as it has for millennia. If the global economy crashes, the cars would run out of gas and be parked and the olives would still grow.

Stone monuments, tombs and cities litter the countryside hereabouts, their edges softened by age, their inscriptions worn and unintelligible. One of the oldest senate buildings ever constructed lies in nearby hills, a tumbledown pile of stone until the restorers got to work and turned it into a beautiful replica of its former glory and a tourist attraction. This seat of government was once the heart of a proud city, now mostly broken stone and a field where goats graze. Monuments crumble and stone wears away. Bureaucracies, governments, presidents, kings—all are ephemeral, all shouting into the wind of their greatness and power. Only the people remain, nurturing their goats and chickens, planting their gardens, their olives and grapes, a great river of humanity rising and falling with tides and currents, but flowing on, enduring.

We can't all return to the village. Nor would we all want to. But we can create a global village of interdependence and understanding. Many who read the *Tao Te Ching* interpret it to mean that one must be a mountain hermit and live in a cave to understand the Tao and to experience the true nature of life. Withdrawal from daily life might be the right thing for some individuals. Doing so is not a universal prescription, however. Lao Tze was not a hermit. He had a long and fruitful career dedicated to improving society, married and raised a family and only retired from a busy life when he was very old. During his active life he cared deeply about society and the well-being of his fellows as is evident from his writings.

> *Retire when the work is done. This is the way of heaven.*
> **—Tao Te Ching**

One of the people I know who is with the Tao is a brilliant philosopher, educated, well read, able to discuss Plato and the plays of Euripides knowledgeably, is an exceptional martial artist, a gifted healer, a world traveler, a father and a successful businessman. He also likes single malt scotch. Another friend is a cancer survivor whose daily life continues to be affected by the disease and the surgeries and therapies she underwent. Yet she is one of the most unfailingly cheerful people I've even known. She spends much of her day helping others and fills each day with light and joy. She is fully engaged in life and in the Tao, even though she knows no more about the Tao than anyone who has heard a casual mention of it. Those who are with the Tao have fun, drink wine, laugh with friends, meet new friends, make love and raise children, help their neighbors and do the best they can to make the world a better place for their having been in it. They love life.

Sail around the world in a small boat. Ride a motorcycle across Europe. Climb a mountain. Float down the Amazon on local ferries. Cross the Sahara to visit Timbuktu. Live in an Indian village, or one in China, Turkey, Rwanda or Borneo. Adventure might be dangerous, but routine is lethal and no one gets out of here alive anyway. Go to Africa and see the elephants, hippos and lions and you'll know we must save them from extinction, and you might decide to lend a hand to help them survive. The world is a fine place. But we do not own it. We share it with countless other life forms and we owe them respect. If you do not wish to or cannot travel, stay at home, live fully, plant a tree that will outlive you, get to know your neighbors, greet each day as an adventure and fearlessly do what you can to reach out to others and help to shine the light in dark places. The Internet is a powerful tool; use it to connect with people around the world. Soon you'll find that strangers are only friends you have not yet met. I began the lessons in this book with sight, with vision, for more than one reason. If we can truly *see,* see the nature of our world and all in it, we can find our way, our Tao, and all survive together.

Clinging to the familiar, and to illusionary safety, is a denial of the fundamental nature of the universe. Change is constant. Google a world map of earthquakes; it might surprise you. Daily the earth shifts under our feet. Our planet travels around our sun and our sun is only a part of our solar system, which is a tiny, swirling mote in a constantly moving and expanding universe. Knowing this, how then can we refuse to see that change is life and life is change. We delude ourselves with attempts to find security in safe suburbs and in playing it safe, in taking no chances, in arming ourselves and attempting to be prepared for any possible contingency. But the only security in our universe is to flow with it and be a part of its unfolding mystery.

Although the externals of our world have changed since Lao Tze's time, we haven't changed much. In addition to providing us practical day-to-day survival tools, the Tao shows us a way to live in difficult times and reveals eternal truths. If we truly see into our own hearts, we will love and respect our inner being, our souls, and treat ourselves with respect. If we see ourselves in others, we will have compassion in our hearts rather than fear or hate. We will reach out to our fellows rather than pushing them away or fighting with them. We will help those in need, and in doing so help ourselves and all of our fellows, for we are all connected, all drops of water in life's great river. If we can see even a tiny part of the mystery underlying the natural world we live in, we will approach it and all its creatures with awe, respect and compassion. If we can see our part in the ebb and flow of the universe, we will find humility and know that while we have a place in the universe we are not at its center, and cannot take without giving back. Understanding this we will understand how to live in this universe and in this tumultuous century, that we are where we're supposed to be and it's up to us to be as we can be.

SUGGESTED READING

Capra, Fritjof, *The Tao of Physics: An Exploration of the Parallels Between Modern Physics and Eastern Mysticism*. 5th ed. Boston: Shambhala, 2010.
A bestseller for thirty-five years, this book first examined the parallels between subatomic physics and Taoist mysticism. For Western readers, especially those of a scientific turn of mind, this validation of the Taoist concepts of the universe helps to provide firm footing when exploring both the Tao and physics.

Diamond, Jared, *Collapse: How Societies Choose to Fail or Succeed*. Rev. ed. New York: Penguin, 2011.
Diamond examines patterns of catastrophic societal collapse, and develops a global thesis through historical-cultural narratives, from the collapse of the Polynesian culture on Easter Island to those of the Anasazi and Maya. Required reading for those who want to understand how we can avoid cultural and ecological suicide.

Hawke, Mykel, *Hawke's Green Beret Survival Manual*. Philadelphia: Running Press, 2009.
Hawke, Mykel, *Hawke's Special Forces Survival Handbook: The Portable Guide to Getting Out Alive*. Philadelphia: Running Press, 2011.
Having served in the same unit, Special Forces (although twenty years earlier), some might think I'm biased in favor of Captain Hawke. But I know the training and the material and think I'm being entirely objective in my recommendation of these books. If you want encyclopedic books on worldwide wilderness survival, these are the ones.

Headquarters, Department of the Army. *The U.S. Army Survival Manual (Department of the Army Field Manual 21-76)*.
A how-to of primitive survival, both short and long term, that covers global conditions and has been used effectively by generations of servicemembers.

Hoff, Benjamin, *The Tao of Pooh*. New York: Penguin, 1982.
A whimsical and entertaining explication of Taoist philosophy through the use of the much-loved Pooh characters.

Lao Tze, *Tao Te Ching*.
Available in many different translations, the one by Gia-Fu Feng and Jane English (Random House, 1974) has been a standard for decades. John C. H. Wu's translation (Shambhala, 1990) is available in a pocket-sized edition that will fit in the corner of any ready bag.

McDougall, Christopher, *Born to Run: A Hidden Tribe, Superathletes, and the Greatest Race the World Has Never Seen*. New York: Alfred A. Knopf, 2009.
McDougall takes us into Mexico's Copper Canyon, where the Tarahumara Indians, who routinely run hundreds of miles, have lived in seclusion for centuries, and to science labs where current work is being done on the physiology of running. On a fundamental level, the Tarahumara run in a similar manner to Taoist masters, although they appear to drink a great deal more alcohol than the Taoists. He also adds valuable information to the growing body of work that demonstrates how modern running shoes with elevated heels damage runner's bodies.

Watts, Allan, with Al Chung-Liang Huang, *Tao: The Watercourse Way*. New York: Pantheon, 1975.
A lucid and eloquent discussion of Taoism. Essential reading and an introduction to a fascinating writer and thinker.

Wescott, David, ed., *Primitive Technology: A Book of Earth Skills*. Layton, UT: Gibbs Smith, 1999.
Dave Wescott was director of the Boulder Outdoor Survival School for many years and is a recognized authority on survival with primitive skills. Highly recommended if you're interested in this subject matter.